Why Sacagawea Deserves the Day Off & Other Lessons from the Lewis & Clark Trail

STEPHENIE AMBROSE TUBBS

University of Nebraska Press　　Lincoln and London

"Why Sacagawea Deserves the Day Off" originally appeared in *Columbia: The Magazine of Northwest History* (Winter 2006–7): 3–6, a publication of the Washington State Historical Society.

"Opening Our Ears: Researching the *Lewis and Clark Companion*" was originally presented at the Confluence of Cultures symposium held at the University of Montana (2003) and was published as part of the symposium proceedings.

Library of Congress Cataloging-in-Publication Data
Tubbs, Stephenie Ambrose.
Why Sacagawea deserves the day off and other lessons from the Lewis and Clark Trail / Stephenie Ambrose Tubbs.
    p. cm.
Includes bibliographical references.
ISBN 978-0-8032-1585-6 (pbk.: alk. paper)
1. Lewis and Clark National Historic Trail—Description and travel. 2. West (U.S.)—Description and travel. 3. Lewis and Clark Expedition (1804–1806)
4. West (U.S.)—Discovery and exploration. 5. United States—Territorial expansion—History—19th century. 6. Tubbs, Stephenie Ambrose—Travel—Lewis and Clark National Historic Trail. I. Title.
F592.7.T834 2008   917.804′2—dc22
2008013453

Set in Adobe Caslon Pro. Designed by A. Shahan.

For all the members of the Charbonneau
Society; the men who follow the women
who follow Lewis and Clark, especially John,
Alex, and Riley Tubbs; and for the ever-loyal
four-legged members of the Seaman Society,
with gratitude and love.

Contents

Acknowledgments

Thanks to the Lewis and Clark Trail Heritage Foundation, Jim Merritt, Landon Jones, Edie Ambrose, Wendy Raney, Phyllis Yeager, Mil and Clay Jenkinson, Dave Borlaug, Amy Mossett, Dayton Duncan, Harry Fritz, Lou Bahin, and David Nicandri for their advice and good counsel. I am indebted to Stephen Barnett for his keen eye and insightful reading of the manuscript.

Thanks to John for suffering through my inconsistent word processing with hardly a complaint and to Alex and Riley for reminding me not to take myself too seriously, and thanks, Mom, for always, always giving me the AST high-five when I needed it.

Introduction

The book you are about to launch into has its roots in a previous publication, an attempt to compile an encyclopedia of people, places, and things associated with the Lewis and Clark Expedition. As it took form, I imagined it might be used as a sourcebook for a novelist or filmmaker or perhaps even a mystery writer. The journals and letters of Lewis and Clark present an endless supply of interwoven threads of minute detail, interesting characters, Native encounters, and geographically diverse scenery that continue to inspire performance art and speculative literature, not to mention road trips, some two hundred years later. Because the alphabetical entries included in our compilation were limited to just the facts, I could not resist the temptation, as I promoted the work, to add my own two cents to the questions posed by Lewis and Clark and our commemoration of their journey. As you will see, at points I restate my opinions and at others I change my mind. Largely that is because I did not write these essays with the intention of publishing them as a collection. Rather, I tried to pick the topics I was most interested in and assemble the arguments that most fascinated me. I then presented them to audiences along the trail who would be familiar enough with the basics of the expedition that they were ready to go past what was written in the journals and follow me beyond the boundaries of conventional history.

Many of these chapters began as conversations with other Lewis and Clark torchbearers, usually around a campfire or at one of the many signature event presentations I attended during the bicentennial. The essays represent my best answer to the puzzle of the Lewis and Clark adventure and why it continues to draw us in even after the hoopla of the two hundredth anniversary has died down, to questions about leadership, geography (real and imagined), personal achievement, and inquisitiveness. What motivated Thomas Jefferson to send out his agents of discovery to begin with? What were the "mutinous expressions" uttered by one of the men? What happened to the dog? Why did Meriwether Lewis end his own life? These are the questions that keep Lewis and Clark scholars up at night, leafing through their thirteen volumes of Moulton. Fortunately for me I had the opportunity to share my musings with an interested audience who did not hesitate to ask pertinent questions and sparked me to dig deeper into the scholarship associated with Lewis and Clark.

The story of the Corps of Discovery is a tantalizing one much like Homer's *Odyssey*, and the longer you study it the more you realize how much there is to learn. And the lesson never ends: as long as people are seeking the trail and reading the journals, it will continue to instruct us forever. At the end of the bicentennial it occurred to me that I had basically written a book. Several rejection slips later I realized it sorely needed some fine-tuning. Thanks to encouraging words from dear friends and family, I did not give up on finding a publisher. Another stroke of good fortune (Lewis and Clark luck?) for me was a chance encounter with

Gary Dunham of the University of Nebraska Press at Montana's Festival of the Book in Missoula, who responded positively to my humble inquiry, "Are you guys still publishing books about Lewis and Clark?" Several months later I had a contract for a book (with the same outfit that published Moulton) that was 95 percent finished. The hard part was mustering the enthusiasm for repeated readings and editing the essays after four years of nonstop Lewis and Clark activities. The inspiration came from the hardworking citizens and conservation groups who somehow managed to save the Rocky Mountain Front in Montana from future oil and gas exploration. This was a huge victory for the conservation community, and it provided a model for other large-scale conservation projects. It also gave me hope that landmark places along the trail could also be prioritized and protected. If we can capture, through the teaching of this story, the imagination of young people, they will come to love the places that inspire them and will work to protect those places so that their children will also have the chance to appreciate American wildlands and the history that happened there.

My friends Rob Quist and Jack Gladstone wrote a song for the Lewis and Clark Trail Heritage Foundation called "Pass It On," in which they say to "Honor the spirit of the land they walked upon." That is what I hope this book will speak to, the imperative to "pass it on." That is the message Thomas Jefferson wanted to convey in his *Notes on the State of Virginia* and, following his lead, what Captains Lewis and Clark did with their journals. It is what anyone who works with their volumes feels compelled to do. The legacy of the journals is that they continue to be discovered, continue to stir up feelings of wonder and delight, and that they continue to provoke late-night discussions around crackling campfires. I hope these essays live up to that tremendous legacy and that my children and yours have the chance to experience both the pleasingly beautiful and the sublimely grand landscape that is the Lewis and Clark Trail.

1. Experiences of a Writer on the Lewis and Clark Trail

My experiences as a writer on the Lewis and Clark Trail stretch out over all of my adult life and some of my childhood. I've been a teenager cartwheeling my way along the trail; an employee of a tour operation working at the Gates of the Mountains on the Missouri River, where I met and later married my husband; and a young mother trepidatious at her young sons leaning out over the edge of a precipice to get a better view. Now as the mother of nearly grown sons, I find myself searching for ways to make the story of the Corps of Discovery relevant to their lives—to teach them to see beyond the many distractions of youth in the twenty-first century and to appreciate and know about one of the greatest journeys in our country's history.

I remember vividly how the whole crazy idea of following a trail for an entire summer was not the most appealing plan to me as a sixteen-year-old city girl. I know this because my journal from that summer is a chronicle of my evolution from a whiny, self-absorbed teen-ager to an off-road traveler coming to love the gypsy life and to appreciate the rigors of hiking, canoeing, and camping. My journal is filled with the kind of memorabilia you would expect: poems, song lyrics, snapshots, and even newspaper clippings of my favorite star of that year's Summer Olympics. The cover of it has drawings, doodles, and a fortune from Bazooka bubble-gum that Lewis and Clark might have appreciated: "Become a mountain climber and you will reach your peak." Although my journal covers only one summer, the trail is very much a part of my present. It remains familiar and all around me. I am lucky to be friends with many of the folks who tell its story and who keep it alive in the minds of young people.

On Kings Hill in central Montana we faced our own version of the sinking of the iron boat when our Chevy truck broke down. First I should explain that from infancy my siblings and I were raised to have an unwavering faith in the Chevy pickup truck. Much like Jefferson and Lewis trusted the technology and the in-genuity of their iron boat, we ranked Chevys right up there with Mom and Dwight Eisenhower for reliability. So when the be-loved Chevy truck broke down, our reaction ranged from disbelief to a refusal to witness its being towed away to the nearest dealer. I recorded on that day that we met the ranger Buzz Adolphson, of Monarch, Montana, friendly, bearded, and sporting a handle-bar moustache, who also happened to be a Lewis and Clark fan and liked the idea of a family following the trail. He hosted us at his cabin for dinner that night and regaled us with stories of what it was like to be a Montana ranger. I told him someday my journal might be published, and he teased me that it would be a bestseller only if I did not put my picture on the cover. Twenty-three years later, I stuck a newspaper clipping alongside that day's entry: a picture of Buzz, still bearded but a bit greyer, patiently "modernizing" the campground on King's Hill.

The Missouri River Breaks National Monument paddle is an adventure that is never the same twice. A most memorable trip was in 1993 with Larry and Bonnie Cook on their boat the *West Wind*. On that particular trip we also had our canoes, but if the wind came up the plan was that we could all ride on their motorized boat and haul the canoes behind. It was a great plan except for one hitch: Bonnie did not want dogs on the barge, and if you have ever been on the Missouri River with Bonnie Cook you know you do not want to rock her boat. We made the mistake of bringing two dogs with us, our old golden retriever, Curly, and our toy poodle named Stanzie. That meant someone had to paddle the dogs in the canoes to the pull-off we had settled on that morning. I will never forget the extreme sense of embarrassment my husband, John, and I felt as we paddled hard and long, eventually past some local fishermen on the bank who exclaimed, "There is a goddamned poodle in that canoe!" Bonnie finally came around, though: she got quite a kick out of the golden retriever swimming out to catch some leftover spaghetti noodles she had thrown overboard. I know I had her laughing when later I sent her a Christmas card that read, "Citizens for a poodle-free Montana." If you write about Lewis and Clark it is mandatory to include at least one good dog story.

As an aside I would like to thank our dear friend Dayton Duncan for making Curly a minor celebrity in Lewis and Clark circles. Dayton described Curly's ascent to the Hole in the Wall and the Needle's Eye in his book *Out West*. Curly is also remembered for throwing up in a canoe as it went over Roundup Rapids on the Big Blackfoot River, but that is another story. According to Dayton, Curly was the first retriever ever to have visited the two landmarks on the same day, an achievement that was not without some protest on the dog's part. I do not know if Dayton can verify that fact, but it sounds likely to me.

Another experience with outfitters came on the Lolo Trail with Harlan and Barb Opdahl. When I was a teenager hiking the Lolo, I always wished we could have done it on horses. Years later, in 1993, when we actually did it on horses, I was surprised to find myself on the second or third day opting to ride in the truck rather than saddling up. Covering the rugged Bitterroot Mountains, the Lolo Trail is intersected with logging roads or, rather, with one-lane dirt roads that have rock on one side and sheer dropoffs on the other. I was with Barb when she had to back her truck, overflowing with gear, down such a road and basically refused to do it. Harlan had to get in and take the wheel. It was the one time I saw him get mad. But I don't blame Barb; I'd rather face an angry husband than back down a logging road any day. Harlan always had a soft spot for my boys, though. He gave them their choice of mounts and told me, as he watched my face go pale, that I had no cause for worry. Mind you they were aged three and six and were in no way experienced riders. I will never forget him carrying my tuckered-out three-year-old, Riley, as Harlan rode his trusty horse Kid with Riley sleeping peacefully in his arms. We have met many special people along the trail, and Larry, Bonnie, Harlan, and Barb rank right up there at the top.

We have also had our share of "greenhorn" experiences. I remember a particular student who came with us one summer on the Lolo Trail. The instructions were to bring quantities of rice, beans, and other easily packed foods they could transport in the car and later bag up for backpacking. Instead of downsizing his supplies, one student packed a ten-pound bag of rice over the trail. When he realized he made a mistake, he thought he could avoid ridicule by putting a small hole in the rice bag about halfway up. He left a trail of rice kernels all the rest of the way. It reminded me of Hansel and Gretel.

Another time a young city slicker and his female friend came with us over Lemhi Pass. Their little Toyota had a hard time in the "gumbo," also known as Montana mud, and they basically made their way sideways up to the top of the pass. When they finally came into camp they were surprised to find that at Lemhi, everyone needed to haul in their own water. They hadn't thought of that. To make matters worse they forgot to pack coats and later lost their keys. They also nearly drowned at the Three Forks after we broke the rule about putting two inexperienced flatlanders in the same canoe. They remained in good spirits, though, and recall the trip fondly to this day.

A few summers ago I was on the river again, near the breaks, this time with forty-five or so youth range campers (rural kids aged twelve to sixteen) in the hundred-degree heat with thirty canoes and only a few campers who knew how to paddle. At one point our canoes were stretched out on the river for at least a mile and a half. The nature walks and readings the camp counselors had scheduled, and which I was to participate in, were hard, if not impossible, to undertake. Not only was it one hundred degrees, but the mosquitoes were very troublesome to say the least. At one point I had to sit in the canoe and read to them about Lewis and Clark as the campers sat in the river to avoid heat exhaustion. A truck stopped on the other side of the river to wonder at the sight. The people in it probably thought we were performing some kind of religious ritual, which in a way we were.

So what is it about the Lewis and Clark Trail that affected my writing? I learned to be observant and to note the extremes—the quirky details—and to hold on to and record the humorous episodes by keeping a daily journal, which though surely subjective is more reliable than my faulty memory. I learned to record the friendships and the characters large and small. I learned that you have to "walk the walk" if you are going to "talk the talk": that nothing can substitute for experiencing the trail for yourself.

I learned that the story of Lewis and Clark is also the story of friendship, helpfulness, proceeding on, and finally reaching the moment of "Ocian in View. O the Joy!"

I have many other stories. I am likely one of the few people who can say she got married on the Lewis and Clark Trial. I once hiked on the Lolo Trail in bare feet because my hiking boots, or "waffle stompers" as we called them, were giving me blisters. I have cooked and eaten boudin blanc, and I do not recommend it. I have explored the Judith River and come to appreciate why Clark named it in honor of the one he loved. Each summer my sons jump into the Missouri River from a thirty-foot cliff at the Gates of the Mountains, just for the fun of it, and of course to scare their mother to death. It has been twenty-eight years since my first experience as a writer on the Lewis and Clark Trail, and I can honestly say that it never gets old for me. The trail, like the river, is very much a living thing. It offers us a way to connect to the past, present, and future. I have always thought that when I reach my paddle forward and pull, the river and I are singing to each other in a language unspoken but which sings, "Just keep rolling along."

2. Missouri River

If there is one thing I share with the residents of the city of Great Falls, Montana, it is a love for the Missouri River—Mighty Mo, Old Misery. I am intimately familiar with this river, and in many ways I grew up on it. I was married on it; every summer my sons insist on diving into it from frighteningly high cliffs, and I have swum in its headwaters and prayed at its falls.

I know that the lessons it teaches are infinite and that the importance of this river to our nation cannot be over-emphasized. Every day our newspapers offer stories about the tug of war going on between the upper Missouri states and the lower ones, between one set of criteria and another regarding proper management. It should be no surprise. I firmly believe the Missouri River will always be in the news.

The following observations paint a portrait of the river. I think they show our relationship to its wildness and its arbitrariness and why it will never be completely tamed. Most of all the Missouri River represents a connection to places beyond our imaginations.

In *Rivers of Change*, Tom Mullen recalls a story of a sixteen-year-old boy from Nebraska City, Nebraska, who put his name and address on a piece of paper and put in into a Coke bottle that he then threw into the Missouri. A year later he received a letter from a sixteen-year-old girl who found his bottle near Downpatrick, Northern Ireland.[1]

Recall that the Missouri was used as a travel corridor long before Lewis and Clark arrived in 1804. Many tribal accounts focus on the Missouri, including creation stories and long-held traditional beliefs about the origins of certain species. All of these stories acknowledge the power of the river, but they are by no means the only testimonials to its strength and tenacity. As the succession of frontiers followed in the wake of the Corps of Discovery, the vagaries of the Missouri remained a major factor in the success or failure of trappers, steamboats, miners, and homesteaders. By 1890 the steamboat era yielded to the railroads but not before some 400 steamboats sank on the Mighty Mo, 250 of those between the years 1819 and 1897.

At 2,540 miles the Missouri is the longest river on the North American continent and the major tributary of the Mississippi River. As naturalist Daniel Botkin writes in *Passage of Discovery*, it drains the Great Plains, an area that makes up one-third of the United States. It draws waters from as high as fourteen thousand feet in the Rockies and deposits them in St. Louis at four hundred feet above sea level.[2] Combined with the Mississippi River, it would be the third-longest river in the world.

From the beginning of his knowledge of it, Thomas Jefferson viewed the Missouri as a source of tremendous potential for commercial exploitation. He thought that the Missouri would afford an easier and therefore more profitable route to the upper Midwest and Northwest than the one the British had already established in Canada, and that the river would be a great connecting link to new markets and resources. He fantasized that the land around the Missouri might harbor mammoths and contain huge mountains of salt. In 1803 Jefferson sent Lewis and Clark to survey his new purchase with the specific instructions to explore the Missouri or any other river "which may offer the most direct & practicable water communication across this continent for purposes of commerce."[3]

What they found was not exactly Jefferson's dream come true, but it did offer the promise of future opportunities for profitable commerce. They mapped the river that would be the vital lifeline in the development of those opportunities. Anyone who has observed the vagaries of the Mighty Missouri can attest to its many moods and the effects those moods have on witnesses.

Historian and Missouri River authority Stanley Vestal writes, "The Missouri was first of all a highway, and it is a highway that has captured the imagination of mankind—a perilous trail leading from Mississippi Swamps to the snow peaks of the Rockies; a trail passing from the warm south to a country bleak and cold and bare as Siberia." He goes on to write that for the folks who lived along the river, the hazards included "cold and wet and violent storms, beating hail and caving banks, snags and rapids, and wrecked boats, an avalanche of high water sweeping all before it." He quotes humorist and journalist George Fitch: "There is only one river that goes traveling sidewise, that interferes in politics, rearranges geography and dabbles in real estate; a river that plays hide and seek with you today and tomorrow follows you around like a pet dog with a dynamite cracker tied to his tail. That river is the Missouri." Vestal also quotes a riverboat operator as saying that "some people think it was just a plain river running along in its bed at the same speed; but it ain't. The river runs crooked through the valley; and just the same way a channel runs crooked through the river . . . the crookedness you can see ain't half the crookedness there is."[4]

Artist George Catlin describes the river by saying, "Almost every island and sand-bar is covered with huge piles of these floating trees, and when the river is flooded, its surface is almost literally covered with floating raft and drift wood which bid positive defiance to keel-boats and steamers on their way up the river. With what propriety this 'Hell of waters' might be denominated the 'River Styx' I will not undertake to decide; but nothing could be more appropriate or innocent than to call it the River of Sticks."[5]

Daniel Botkin, in *Passage of Discovery*, writes, "On the surface of our planet, the Missouri River acts as an irresistible force against which there is no immovable object. All earthly things that confront the Missouri, all attempts to surround it, to seize it and hold it back, give way. If not now then later. The mountains fall before it as do the more meager works of mankind—levees, houses, and bridges."[6]

Strode Hinds finds this statement by Fitch in an early account: "The Missouri cuts corners, runs around at night, lunches on levees, and swallows islands and small villages for dessert. It makes farming as fascinating as gambling. You never know whether you are going to harvest corn or catfish."[7]

Gordon Young writes in *National Geographic*, "I recalled a tale about an old farmer who ran Missouri River water through a pipe and sawed it into disks when it came out—for grindstones."[8]

As early settlers said of the Missouri and other western rivers, "Too thick to drink, too thin to plow."

Fitch, in 1907, writes that "A steamer that cannot, on occasion, climb a steep clay bank, go across a cornfield and corner a river that is trying to get away, has little excuse for trying to navigate the Missouri." Of its legendary hunger he said, "The Missouri eats eighty acres at a mouthful and picks its teeth with the embers of a great red barn."[9]

Captain William Clark wrote, "The water we drink, or the Common water of the Missourie at this time, contains half a Comn Wine Glass of ooze or mud to every pint" Describing the meanderings from the shore, Clark wrote that "in Pursueing Some Turkeys I struck the river twelve miles below within 370 yards."[10]

Captain Meriwether Lewis commented, "This immence river so far as we have yet ascended, waters one of the fairest portions of the globe, nor do I believe that there is in the universe a similar extent of country, equally fertile, well watered, and intersected by such a number of navigable streams."[11]

President Thomas Jefferson called the Missouri "in fact, the principal river, contributing more to the common stream than does the Mississippi, even after its junction with the Illinois."[12]

William Least Heat Moon, in his *River Horse*, wrote that "given the American mania for rankings, the United States could still have today—even after the shortenings—the third longest river in the world simply by dropping three letters and changing three others to make Mississippi spell Missouri. Failing that, then perhaps a grand compromise: the Missourippi. Try it: Mizza-rippi."[13]

After exploring the Mississippi in the early 1720s the French explorer Father Pierre Francois de Charlevoix observed that "I believe this is the finest confluence in the world. The two rivers are much the same breadth each about a half a league; but the Missouri is by far the most rapid and seems to enter the Mississippi like a conqueror."[14]

And Gordon Young tells us, "I hurried downstream to witness a marriage. Old Misery becomes one with Old Man River—the Mississippi—just north of St. Louis. Like a dutiful wife she assumes her husband's name. The Missouri is no more. I was sorry to lose her. Our acquaintanceship had been close enough to reveal glimpses of her magnificently cantankerous personality. All of our dams and turbines and revetments have not tamed her completely."[15]

Of the original river only about one-third of it still flows freely. It is now a hundred miles shorter than when Lewis and Clark proceeded on.

In terms of my own personal observations, I will say that the Missouri River Breaks is one of the wildest parts of the river. I have canoed it when we were in the river more than on it because of the extreme heat. I have paddled it wearing every stitch of clothing I had with me because it was so cold and the wind was blowing so hard at our backs. We called that episode the "Missouri River Sleigh Ride" because we made more miles than we ever had before. I have seen it rain, hail, and blow like a hurricane.

Canoeing in the Gates of the Mountains depends on the weather and the wind. A headwind when exiting the Gates of the Mountains canyon is definitely something to be avoided. My sister Grace and I once faced headwinds in a canoe loaded with gear. She was about twelve and I was sixteen. We had been following our parents' canoe and decided to duck into a little side bay to take a break from the wind. When our parents turned around to check on us, they could not see us, and for a few agonizing moments they presumed us drowned, which was not a far-fetched conclusion at that point. Another time at the Gates of the Mountains we watched a forest fire jump the river. Once, when the water level had been lowered at the dam, the river returned to its natural channel, and we walked on the bottom of the lake and found all sorts of long-lost fishing gear.

For me, the town of Fort Benton represents the quintessential river town. From my first visit there in 1976 I felt the small-town community spirit, admired the magnificent city park and riverfront, and enjoyed the friendliness of everyone we met. I still love to visit Fort Benton, especially in the early summer when the big cottonwoods send their fluffy seeds into the air. If you visit and notice a bench along the river you will see that it was placed there in honor of the famous local outfitter Bob Singer, whom we were lucky to float with. He knew more about the river than anyone and always loved to share his stories about it around the campfire. I think the bench is a perfect tribute to Bob and his spirit and to the town that loved him so.

I know several people who believe in river gods, especially in the case of the Missouri River. They tell of boaters who poured oil into the river and later broke down and had to be towed back to the marina. The Missouri has a strong karma, they tell me.

My love for the Missouri has much to do with characters like Bob Singer. The more I travel its course the more I feel I have to come back next year. There are always new things to learn and new things to see, new characters to run into and old friends to get reacquainted with. I see the Missouri River as a living and vital thing that connects us to people and places far from home. Imagine finding a bottle in Ireland from a boy in Nebraska, brought there by the mysterious, ever-winding, and ultimately unconquered Mighty Mo.

3. Paddling into Bodmer

As we launched our little fleet at Coal Banks Landing I was under the extreme misconception that I had seen it all. After more than twenty-five years of paddling the Missouri River I imagined I had weathered every trial the Mighty Mo could hurl at me. Heck, I had even written and spoken publicly about how it was never the same trip twice and how you had to be prepared for every kind of extreme when you paddle the last undeveloped stretch of the river, the 148-mile Upper Missouri River Breaks National Monument—no matter what the weather forecasters in Great Falls said.

Our trip started routinely enough. We gathered for drinks and dinner at the magnificently restored Grand Union Hotel in Fort Benton, Montana, a town currently experiencing a mild economic boom and which proudly displays its rich steamboat, fur trade, and homesteader history in several small museums and interpretive areas. Some might call it a sleepy town, but to me Fort Benton is alive with activity, and it has grown substantially in the last decade.

The trip was scheduled to take two and a half days through the White Cliffs section of the monument. According to the Monument Proclamation it contains "a spectacular array of biological, geological and historical objects of interest." For a more vivid description turn to the journals of Lewis and Clark on May 31, 1805, where Meriwether Lewis wrote of scenes exactly as they appear today:

the thin stratas of hard freestone intermixed with the soft sandstone seems to have aided the water in forming this curious scenery. As we passed on it seemed as if those seens of visionary inchantment would never have and end; for here it is too that nature presents to the view of the traveler vast ranges of walls of tolerable workmanship, so perfect indeed are those walls that I should have thought that nature had attempted here to rival the human art of masonry had I not recollected that she had first began her work.

To say it is remote is accurate but hardly makes the point. If you break down in this area you better have a backup plan, and once you launch your boats, do not expect any kind of escape until you pull out at Judith Landing some fifty winding miles downriver, still at least a hundred road miles from the nearest hospital. Outfitters tell of helicopter rescues but I find it best not to contemplate such scenarios. Suffice it to say you want to pack light and carefully. One overlooked item could mean a night of total misery, and you never know what item will become indispensable. Over the years I learned the lesson of rain gear—ALWAYS BRING IT—no matter how nice the weather seems when you launch. On this trip I remembered, luckily, to throw in some rain pants and paddling gloves. Sometimes the smallest thing can make a difference. The problem, for you novices, is that if you pack too lightly inevitably weather will come in and you will freeze. Or, if you pack too much you end up not needing half the articles in your dry bag, which you still have to haul up the side of steep, muddy banks. The trick is to pack just enough to achieve the "Zen" of packing for a river trip. It is all about finding a happy medium between hot and cold, wet and dry. Packing successfully for a river trip is a lesson in life. Because I was making this particular trip for business, my services as a Lewis and Clark enthusiast would be put to the test, so naturally I packed too many books and maps. But I did pack a good pair of brand-new river shoes, which turned out to be one of the best things I could have had.

I imagined this trip would be a breeze because of the luxury of having experienced and knowledgeable outfitters. Ours could not have been better humored or more agreeable. They set up and took down our tents, fed us exceedingly well, and provided air mattresses, libations, and crackling fires at night. They also had that most magical invention of Western civilization: the propane heater, which can come in very handy at times.

They brewed good strong camp coffee in the mornings and served it with hearty western breakfasts and, most appreciated of all, hot water for the tea drinkers. Mostly they established a swift and efficient camping machine for the duration of the trip.

The first night we camped at Eagle Creek. Even though it was already filled with campers when we arrived, our outfitters managed to secure some decent tent sites. That evening we hiked back into what they call Slot Canyon, a sandstone maze of freaky formations that seems to get narrower as it winds its way around until you come out on top to a dizzying view of the river below. On this hike a great horned owl regarded us more or less as if we were noisy neighbors. It reminded me of a previous encounter, years ago on that same stretch of river, with a pair of bighorn sheep. They had gazed down at us from the cliffs as if to say, "You may pass, but make it quick."

That evening when the clouds rolled in and rain started pelting our tents, most went to bed early, but a few of us stayed up and told stories under the tarp set up for the kitchen. We raised our glasses and toasted to a good day's progress tomorrow.

The second day we needed to make roughly twice the distance we paddled on the first. We all seemed content with our previous day's canoeing partners. I noticed no one even switching seats. I liked our canoe, a fiberglass "clipper" that the outfitter said was the fastest in his fleet. I figured he was teasing me, but it turned out we were among the first to make it into camp each day despite being fully loaded with gear. One of things that made this trip memorable was that I finally got to take the stern.

Taking the stern is a huge responsibility, even in a river as deceptively easy to paddle as the Missouri. In our family the stern is usually a job for the strongest males, but in the case of this trip my canoeing experience outweighed that of most of our party, male or not. For my bowman I chose J. E., a Gulf Coast resident and Katrina survivor who had never canoed a day in his life. His qualifications for the bow, however, were outstanding: a lifelong athlete, health club owner, Mississippi State football coach, and southern charmer extraordinaire. He is hard of hearing in one ear so we did not spend a lot of time idly chit-chatting. Consequently I heard more river sounds on that trip than ever before, including the amazing sound of the air going through the wings of a pelican as it flew overhead. J. E. was also a mischievous cajoler who would tell everyone when we stopped that he was doing all the paddling and I was just looking at the scenery. As anyone with canoeing experience can tell you, in some ways this is true. The bow is the motor, and while the stern has to paddle, too, they must also do a lot of ruddering, j-stroking, and steering the boat to maintain the most desirable line down the river. I found that since this trip, I like the stern very much; in fact I may never give it up. You have all the power and the challenge of more than just reaching forward, pulling, and stroking . . . you have the wheel! You are the decider! And so on our second day I again took the stern, and we loaded up onto the same swift boat the second day as well.

That morning I climbed to a nearby overlook and surveyed our beautiful little encampment at the base of what used to be called the Eye of the Needle formation. It no longer exists, some say because of vandalism, others say just because of the natural order of things in the Breaks. From my vantage point I got an eyeful of dark, gray, threatening skies in every direction. In Montana we rarely get the kind of rain that lasts all day, but this looked like it had potential. I mentioned to one of the outfitters that it looked like we would need every stitch of rain gear, including his extras. He agreed with a wink: "This ain't my first rodeo, sister."

The problem was that we had a few folks in danger of going hypothermic if it turned cold. Inadequate rain gear can suddenly go from being a minor inconvenience to a life-threatening situation in the Missouri River Breaks if the wind picks up and comes in from the north. Luckily the temps stayed relatively warm, with a light wind and only a drizzle, what my Irish grandfather would call a fine soft rain. That would soon change. Our plan was to paddle for the Hole in the Wall—also known as Pierced Rock, formed as wind eroded the sandstone into a hole big enough for several people to stand in—and have lunch and, weather permitting, hike up to the Hole. We made it there in good time. The steady drizzle made us dig in and paddle hard. By the time we stopped for lunch it actually seemed to be clearing. Better yet, the paddling kept us warm. We hiked up to the Hole for a view of the river in both directions that puts your speck-on-this-earth existence into proper perspective and at the same time offers one of the best group photo ops on the entire Missouri. The hike also kept us warm while we ate a fine lunch. I found it interesting how warm the water felt at this point, like a warm bath. I considered going in for a swim but I had all of my rain gear on and was not particularly cold. The warmth of the river stayed in the back of my mind the rest of the day. It seemed sort of like a river safety net.

We didn't linger after lunch. Extra gear was handed out, including duct tape and wool hats. Several of our party were shivering even though it wasn't really raining yet; it was just that we had never had a chance to completely dry out. We were damp and in need of a good fire and a hot cup of tea but no one complained or said they wanted to quit. What good would that do? We were determined. Or maybe we were just resigned to our fate: it was going to rain hard and we were going to get wet. The outfitters hit the river in high gear to get downriver to set up our next camp. "We'll make a fire for when you get in," they called as they took off. "Make it a big one!" I yelled back.

That afternoon would turn out to be the wettest, most uncomfortable, disagreeable, and dangerous (thanks to numerous nearby lightning strikes) time on the Missouri I ever endured. Yet in many ways it was the most uplifting experience as well. I came to understand what Captain Clark meant when he advised one of his sons to practice what he called "contentment of situation."

As we pulled out of our Hole in the Wall lunch spot, I looked back at our canoes strewn haphazardly behind us in the river and thought that, except for our boats, it looked just like we were paddling into a Bodmer masterpiece: the faded light, the misty lens effect, the dark hue of the sandstone. I told myself I would never forget this scene no matter how wet I got later. Besides, it was no use trying to pull out my digital camera. It would have to be the kind of Kodak moment one files in the Missouri River Breaks memory bank to pull out whenever viewing one of Bodmer's works.

As we proceeded on and water slowly seeped down the back of my neck and down the sleeves of my rain jacket, we noticed that the side creeks and gullies were bank-full with milky gray runoff that produced an interesting acoustic of running water echoed by the cliffs. It was loud, a sound I never heard before. Large boulders of sand called cannonballs rolled along underneath our boats. We were also being treated to a fine lesson in the making of this remarkable segment of river, witnessing how it came to be that the formations looked the way they did and why banks had sloughed off and fallen into the river.

During the most intense downpour, when the lightning was cracking around us, I thought about the proper sort of respect to show in such a situation. I have known a few silly people who like to wave their paddles at the sky and proclaim, "Is that the best you can do? Rain harder! Make it rain harder! Come on, show me what you've got!"

Perhaps because I have known hurricanes, hailstorms, blizzards, and some God-awful storms on this very stretch of river, my reaction is quite the opposite. I try to make myself very small, murmur prayers, and ask the Great Spirit, "What have I done to offend thee?" then wait for an answer. In this case it was easy. This kind of rain in Montana, a state enduring its seventh year of drought, is truly a blessing. In the words of Bob Marley, "Everything is gonna be alright," or at least that is what I kept telling myself. I let the outfitters worry about the particulars, like whether the roads out of Judith Landing would be passable when we pulled in there the next day.

Then something miraculous happened. The rain stopped and the sun came out. "Here comes the sun! It's alright!" And when we got to camp we had shelter—dry tents and the ability to dry our gear (thanks, Propane Guy!) and hot tea and later fine wine and cold beer. Just as we landed, a large boulder splashed into the river from the opposite bank and we all cheered. I took it as a good omen. As our party staggered in with stories of constant bailing, still for the most part drenched to the bone, there was another common refrain: "We did it." Just like Lewis and Clark.

Well maybe not *just* like Lewis and Clark, but at least enough like them that we would all feel proud of ourselves for several days and maybe more. And we might appreciate just a fraction more what they must have felt: there is no escape . . . moving forward is the only option. There is no turning back. As they say in Montana, "Never say whoa in a mud hole," which I always regarded as a worthy philosophy of life.

And best and perhaps most magical and transforming of all, we had the distinct pleasure of having a fiddler and two of her most precious and sweet-sounding—and dry!—fiddles she would play for us around a warm fire. Our merrily disposed crew enjoyed a moment of high hilarity (and for another, stunned silence) when one of the group dropped a very lifelike rattlesnake into the circle around the fire. The reaction was swift. A few warned the victim not to move, and one of the outfitters grabbed a log and beat that poor artificial snake to bits. So what could have produced screams and possibly fainting spells instead elicited giggles and stunned expressions such as "Wow, that was pretty good."

But back to the fiddle. I now know what a fiddle and a fiddler meant to the Corps of Discovery. I know how the sounds echo off the walls of the white cliffs with coyotes chiming in close by. I know what it means to look up and see a shooting star and hear a familiar fiddle tune at the same time, after facing all that Nature could dish out with only contentment of situation in mind. I vowed to make that trip annually for the rest of my life. It never fails to affect me profoundly, even without the fiddles. I come off the river and no matter how tired I am, I feel rejuvenated, fine-tuned, newly strung, refiddled. I feel like I want to go on. I feel like I want to come back and do it again with all my best friends. I always feel like I have to come back.

Of course it helps having outfitters who provide appetizers of proscuitto and figs, mozzarella and gourmet olives, not to mention sumptuous main courses and delicious desserts with fine wine and cold beer, who set up sheltered areas to warm and dry our wet and sundry items, and who cheerfully want to banter and B.S. with anyone who will listen. I heard one say in response to what he does in the "off" season, "I'm in construction so I can ski all winter, and I'm outfitting so I can paddle rivers all summer. I basically make just enough to support my habit of living the outdoor life in Montana, and I wouldn't have it any other way." No wonder I love these guys.

I met another Montana paddler recently who told me, as he was launching into the Clark Fork, that his doctor had prescribed three canoe trips per week. "He gave me the choice: paddling or happy pills, and you can see which I prefer!"

Our last day was easy. No high drama from the weather gods, and in fact it was exceedingly hot and blindingly bright. This was a day for serious SPF application. After what we faced the previous day everyone got on the river with a strong sense of confidence that fueled us on to our pull-out spot at Judith Landing: a parking space for shuttle vehicles and a small cabin selling pop. Arriving there, the paddler is reminded just how truly isolated he still is. The nearest town, Big Sandy, is still miles away. And likely your vehicle is farther still. Inevitably when you pull into Judith Landing you begin to understand where the middle of nowhere is.

I have not said much about the composition of our group, other than my bowman, but I will say this, they were all game. No one whined once. In fact it would not be exaggerating to say that many were genuinely curious about what lay below our pull-out spot. They confessed that they wanted to proceed on. I tried to think of the words they would use to describe the past two days to their friends. My hunches were confirmed when one told me later that his daughter was envious and told him, "Dad that sounds so awesome!"

So this trip, which I presumed would be fairly routine and all business, turned out instead to be a life-affirming adventure. I learned once again to never take any single piece of gear for granted, including a sponge for bailing out your boat, and to always go with a good outfitter for comfort and sometimes survival's sake, and to always include an able fiddle player in the party. It is impossible to listen to a fiddle on the banks of the Missouri without being moved, no matter how wet your clothing is. And to have it played for you as we did, as a wake-up call backed up by the melodious song of the meadowlark. As the cowboys say, "That is as close to heaven as anyone can be on this earth."

On our final turn into Judith Landing we could see a large horse herd above us on the bank. It reminded me of the feeling Lewis and Clark describe when they saw domestic cattle on the return part of their journey. In this case it was the horses who signaled our return to civilization. Recalling my childhood days spent horse worshipping I clicked my tongue and called to them the way cowboys do. Surprisingly, it worked. A fine mare and her foal came down the bank and stepped into the river to regard me as if to ask, "Who are you?" I channeled my answer to her: "I am a Montana woman and I just paddled into Bodmer, and I did it in the stern."

4. In Search of Perfect Harmony
Keeping an Expedition Happy Now and Then

Think back about your favorite trip. And then think about it in the context of the Lewis and Clark Expedition. Imagine traveling many miles against the current on the Missouri River to get to the Knife River Villages, in present-day North Dakota, and then to arrive and meet new friends and spend the winter there with them, learning all you could about the miles ahead. It is hard for us to conjure what it must have been like to be a member of the expedition. You would have been a soldier, a frontiersman from Kentucky, or a French boatman hired to pull and pole the boats upriver. You might have been hired as interpreter or sign talker, like George Drouillard. During my travels on the trail over the last twenty-seven years I admit it is sometimes hard for me to relate to those men, just as it is also hard for me to relate to the young Shoshone woman who joined the expedition with her husband and newborn son as an interpreter during the expedition's winter at the Knife River Villages.

Try to understand Lewis and Clark by imagining spending two years away from your friends, family, and home. I imagine that it isn't so much the day-to-day grind of getting across the country that would bother me as a woman of the twenty-first century. I suppose I would get used to the constant rowing, towing, poling, wading, pulling, paddling, marching, and riding. It is the lack of distractions that would do me in. I think of us modern-day travelers as not just spoiled by the ease of getting there, but as so short in attention span that we miss most of what we are driving through even during broad daylight. Obviously we travel for different reasons today. Sometimes it seems our aim isn't so much to discover America as it is to discover ourselves.

But what I would really like to examine here is the way the distractions of the trail both in our time and in the captains' time keep us from going completely mad. They enable us to proceed on. Without them we would probably descend into despair. I realized how true this is as I watched a program about famed explorer Earnest Shackelton. When he and his men were trapped on an ice floe for months, the biggest danger was insanity. Shackelton had his men dress up in improvised costumes to perform plays for each other, and he brought all of his men home in good shape. Even Harry Potter has his quidditch.

In our time it is not uncommon to see car advertisements advising us that a TV in the car is the best way to keep children happy during long drives. I cannot argue this as I have never considered having a television in my car. We do go in for NPR and books on tape, and each of my sons has his own CD player and headset, and lately, I confess, we have added cell phones to our baggage; so I am not pretending to be virtuous, but I do think that if one of the men of the expedition witnessed how much we pack in the way of entertainment for our long trips, he would have a good belly laugh and call us all soft in the head. One thing we would agree on, however, is the need for jerky. Lewis and Clark ate a lot of it and so do we. Not only does it stave off hunger, it passes the time, and a mouth busy chewing is less likely to complain, argue, or whine.

When it comes to breaking up the trip, there is nothing like a large, slobbery, usually wet dog (with that distinct odor wet dogs get) to offer distractions. The captains had Seaman, and I have frequently traveled with dogs, and sometimes cats, on the trail. They always take up too much space and shed everywhere, but they are good companions and can usually provide something to laugh about on a long trip. Seaman was a courageous working dog who saved the crew from stampeding buffalo and rampaging grizzly bears. He hunted, brought in fowl, and once even caught an antelope, which impressed Ordway enough to take the time to note the accomplishment in his journal. On the Ohio River, at the beginning of the journey, Seaman fetched in squirrels that were migrating across the river. Imagine him jumping into a sea of squirrels—what fun for a dog! It also pleased his master, for Lewis wrote that "they were fat and I thought them when fried pleasant food."

Our dogs entertained us along the trail, too. Once when we were camped in Kansas, our black lab caught a swimming frog in his mouth. Another time, in the Missouri River Breaks, our golden retriever retrieved some leftover spaghetti noodles the outfitter had thrown overboard. Of course he didn't really retrieve the noodles, he swallowed them in big gulps, but it did provide us all with a good chuckle. I won't go into what happened driving along the Columbia River when my father decided the dogs needed a dose of medicine as we loaded up for the day. Needless to say we laughed about it later, but not so much at the time. (When they needed to, the Corps ate dogs, and all of them, except for Clark, even learned to like it. They purchased dogs from the Indians to eat. While we enjoy hot dogs around the fire, the men of the Lewis and Clark Expedition enjoyed the real thing.)

By our modern standards the men of the Corps of Discovery would have had much to complain about; but if you compare their lives to the lives of their friends back in the states, they did not have it so bad. As my friend Bob Moore points out in his book *Tailor Made and Trail Worn*, a soldier's life was terrible hard, endlessly repetitive, and offered little in the way of decent compensation. Along with constant drills and inspections, men back at the fort were more likely to argue and therefore more likely to receive punishment. The men of the expedition could expect a fair wage and land grants when they returned. Not to mention a chance to avoid the monotony of life at a military post. No wonder these men were happy to take a chance and head up the river to places they had no way of anticipating. They had no idea what to expect, but that was part of the appeal.

They would be learning new skills, seeing new things, and tasting new tastes, which themselves could be considered a diversion. Do not forget that Lewis and Clark packed the first traveling library in the trans–Mississippi West, carrying maps and manuals of astronomy, natural history, and geology. They even carried a set of encyclopedias to the Pacific and back. Several of the men kept journals, but rather than being a diversion, I think that for other than Sergeants Ordway and Gass, this was just another chore to keep up with. It is different for us modern-day journal keepers, as we have the leisure to record the most trivial details and our own feelings. There is little of that in the journals. They recorded the weather, how far they traveled, and what they came across, but not much about how they felt about it. Clark liked to draw or doodle in his journal, and both captains sometimes sketched examples of the remarkable things they were observing. Clark also made a rendering of the layout of Fort Clatsop.

One thing they could expect was a lot of hunting. When you read the journals, starting with the abridged version, it is impossible not to notice the number of times the men are sent out in small groups to hunt. Not surprisingly it was as constant a duty as pulling the boat or gathering wood for the fire. For our modern-day hunters this would qualify as a diversion, since most of the hunters in our time do it for sport, not because they need to put dinner on the table. These men had to do it so often, I sincerely doubt they considered it any fun whatsoever. (They did enjoy the shooting contests they held with the farmers around Wood River.) And when you add territorial grizzly bears and miserable weather conditions to the mix, the idea of doing it for the sheer love of the hunt was probably the farthest thing from their minds. The same can generally be said for fishing, although in one incident following the sinking of the *Experiment*, his iron boat, Lewis does mention that he went fishing. I would say on that day, after that disappointment, fishing must have been a diversion.

As the leaders of the expedition, Meriwether Lewis and William Clark were assigned by President Jefferson to find the easiest route over the mountains to the Pacific Ocean. He assumed, as did most of the learned men of his time, that the river systems in the West would resemble those of the East. This was an unfortunate and incorrect assumption and one which the Lewis and Clark Expedition would ultimately disprove. But they had other tasks, especially in the field of mapmaking and surveying the land they traveled through. Part of the genius of Jefferson is that he picked a man who was up to the task when he chose his old friend and assistant Meriwether Lewis, and then Lewis picked William Clark, who would turn out to be the perfect partner for him in leading the unit. Jefferson believed in writing things down. He believed in measuring, listing, and naming the plants, animals, and landforms that were new or unknown to him. As his agents, Lewis and Clark would frame the West into one big perfectly ordered picture in which the Indians were friendly and helpful and the diplomatic threats from other interested governments faded away into the sunset.

Now if that job sounds daunting—and we can have no doubt that these explorers were busy—imagine the added burden of keeping the family happy, making sure everyone was in what they termed "perfect harmony." Nothing is worse than taking a trip if everyone is grumbly. Which is why I use the word "genius" when it comes to our captains. They knew when the men had had enough and when it was time to take a break. As military officers they knew when to discipline the men and when to let them have a laugh.

Holidays offered the men a chance to remember the festive traditions of home and to bond closer together as a family who would hopefully live to celebrate many more holidays in the years to come. For their first Christmas, in 1803 at Wood River, the men were still feeling out their boundaries with respect to the captains' orders, and there were a few disciplinary problems. Christmas Day started with the men firing a traditional cannon reverie, which woke Captain Clark; he commented in his journal, "Some of the party had got drunk (2 fought) the men frolicked and hunted all day." By the second holiday at Fort Mandan, things were much more civilized. They once more fired the cannon first thing Christmas morning and spent the day "merrily disposed" after raising the flag over their fort for the first time. Sergeant Ordway wrote in his journal, "We had the Best to eat that could be had & continued firing dancing and frolicking dureing the whole day . . . all in peace and quietness."

The day was meant to be a private party, as Ordway notes, "The Savages did not trouble us as we had requested them not to come as it was a Great medician day with us." The men toasted to their fort and flag with taffia, or rum, and spent the remainder of the month, according to Sergeant Gass, in "peace and tranquility."

By their third Christmas together, the crew displayed every evidence of being a true family. Once again the cannons were fired first thing Christmas morning, and this time the men

decided to gather under the window of the newly constructed Fort Clatsop and sing their captains a Christmas carol. In
return the captains divided all of the remaining pipe tobacco
among those who smoked and gave silk handkerchiefs to the
rest. Lewis and Clark exchanged presents, and then several of
the men presented Clark with a special pair of moccasins and
an Indian basket. Sacagawea gave her friend Clark two dozen
white weasel tails, which in some tribes would be worn by a
brave warrior. As Ordway wrote, "We have no ardent Spirits
but are all in good health which we esteem more than all the
ardent Spirits in the world. We have nothing to eat but poore
Elk meat and no Salt to Season that with, but Still keep in good
Spirits as we expect this to be the last winter that we will have
to pass in this way."

They also celebrated the Fourth of July. In 1805 they drank
the last of those ardent spirits to celebrate the anniversary of
the United States. Other events worth celebrating included New
Year's and the captains' birthdays, when they treated themselves
to a special dinner or an extra round of the whiskey ration.

Special treats, in and of themselves, were cause for celebration. During the portage around Great Falls, Captain Lewis once
made "each man a suet dumpling by way of a treat" and added
it to a buffalo jerky stew they feasted on that night. He made
a celebration meal out of white pudding sausage called boudin
blanc; he wrote a long journal entry with the step-by-step recipe
for making such a meal, including the final step, which was to dip
the boudin blanc, "two dips and a flirt," in the Missouri River for
good measure. In October 1805 Private John Collins brewed up
some libation from fermented camas roots. The journals note that
it was "verry good beer." And Sacagawea understood the power of
treats. She gave her brother Cameahwait his first taste of sugar.

Lewis seemed to take extra pleasure in the diversion provided
by a special treat. Among his favorite dishes were beaver tail, buf-

falo hump and tongue, eucholon (anchovies), a good trout, and perhaps a tasty boiled puppy stew.

During my trips along the trail I would say our big treat is the local Dairy Queen. But we also have favorites, including the aforementioned jerky, southern-style red beans, sausage and rice, and above all M&Ms picked out of what someone euphemistically named "trail mix."

We would swap M&Ms at a high price for all of the other junk food we had in our backpacks. Lewis and Clark also swapped food and learned new cooking methods as they met their Native hosts along the trail. They learned how to appreciate and eventually how to prepare many foods in what Lewis called "Indian style." Camas, pemmican, smoked salmon, hog peanuts, Jerusalem artichokes, and wappato roots are just a few of the foods they sampled.

As they proceeded on, the captains and their men also learned about other aspects of Native American culture. It comes as a surprise to some that the Corps actually played games together with the Indians. They ran good-natured foot races and held horse races with the Nez Perce. They tried to learn a complicated version of backgammon that the Clatsop played, but Clark wrote, "I cannot properly understand it." The Shoshone and the Nez Perce, and indeed many tribes, enjoyed a game called the hand game that involved singing and passing sticks and then guessing who held the stick when the singing stopped. Another common game among the Mandan was tchung-kee, or the hoop and pole game. They watched the Mandan women play a spirited version of a hacky sack or football-style game and admired their skill. Several times during the journey, they mention the men playing prisoner's base, a game we would recognize as base or tag.

Campfire stories no doubt seasoned the trip. Here I am not referring to the kind we typically tell around the fire, ghost stories or long-winded versions of urban myths. Their campfire stories probably centered on their own more outrageous exploits: "Remember the time Sacagawea saved the journals from floating downstream?" "Remember the time Captain Lewis almost fell off a cliff?" "How about the time we tried to flush a prairie dog out of his hole in the ground using buckets and buckets of water?" They could talk about when it was forty below at Fort Mandan and they noticed the sun dogs, or that time they saw the whale, or when an Indian dog untied Pryor's canoe, or a beaver chewed down the green pole that contained an important note from Clark to Lewis regarding which river to take near the Three Forks. They could talk about all those buffalo, as far as the eye could see. They could use all of their previous diversions and side trips to entertain themselves on every long, cold night, whether at Fort Clatsop or some lonely spot in the Bitterroot Mountains. During one such side trip, on a miserably hot day in present-day South Dakota, the Corps decided to take a six-mile hike to investigate a spirit mound that, according to the Indians, harbored little devils who would kill them if they came too close. Clark concluded that it was all silly superstition and attributed the stories to swarms of flying ants that attracted flocks of birds. Poor Seaman, the dog, in his heavy black coat had to be sent back to the river because of the heat.

But two things must have especially spiced things up for the men and really made a difference in their esprit d' corps. One must have accompanied the journey as surely as the rivers and streams they traveled on: their music. They carried two fiddles, a tambourine, and what Sergeant Ordway called a "sounden horn." We know Lewis bought "4 tin blowing horns" when he was purchasing supplies in Philadelphia. Pierre Cruzatte, the one-eyed boatman, played the fiddle "extremely well." Some of the Indians they met along the way had instruments of varying kinds and design. In what we would call a cultural exchange, the Corps and the Indians made music together in something like jam sessions and would dance and sing and laugh as they did so. One man, Francois Rivet, got so carried away he would dance on his head or hands and make everyone laugh at the sight. Clark's slave, York, displayed a talent for dancing as well. In one incident a tribe along the Columbia River showed the men their prophet dance, and the men in turn showed the Indians their kind of dancing, perhaps the Virginia reel. It was a perfect harmony in more ways than one. After reaching what Lewis called that long-wished-for spot, the confluence of the Missouri and Yellowstone, in April 1805, he wrote, "We ordered a dram to be issued to each person, this soon produced the fiddle, and they spent the evening with much hilarity, singing and dancing and seemed as perfectly to forget their past toils, as they appeared regardless of those to come."

The fiddle playing also acted as a gesture of peace. Several times Cruzatte brought out the fiddle at the request of the Indians.

I imagine that the music did not stop at night. Traditionally, the engagés, the French boatmen, would sing as they paddled, as much to keep the rhythm of the rowing as to relieve the boredom of the long hours. They might have to sing without the fiddle because they were on the move, but they could whistle and sing their own tunes as they worked. I imagine Sacagawea hummed to her son, and not just at night. Lewis might even have hummed to himself occasionally. We don't know. It is not the sort of thing one notes in a journal. "Spent the afternoon humming to myself," or more likely, "So and so hummed all day. It was most annoying."

As Jefferson instructed, the party was to avoid confrontation with the Indians at all costs: "Assure them you come in Peace," he had ordered. While there are a few notable exceptions, overall the captains followed those orders and went beyond them. They became friends with some of the people they encountered. Men with names like Looking Glass, Twisted Hair, Sheheke, Yellept, Cameahwait, and Comowool—a man the captains liked so much they gave Fort Clatsop to him upon their departure. As material evidence of these friendships, swaps were made and gifts given that went beyond the diplomatic gestures Jefferson required. Lewis received a garment made of ermine or weasel tails known as a tippet from the Shoshone leader Cameahwait. In return Lewis gave him his hat and gun. Robert Frazer once traded an old razor to an elderly Nez Perce woman for two Spanish dollars. Each probably thought they had the better bargain. Once, a Walla Walla chief presented Clark with a white horse. During their stay at Fort Mandan the neighborly visits and exchanges went far beyond what President Jefferson had in mind, but they kept the men happy and contented. Think how unpleasant it would have been for them without friends.

So in my list of diversions I would definitely include music and friendship. We may be able to live without them, but life is so much sweeter if they are part of the mix. Speaking for myself and my own trips and side trips on the Lewis and Clark Trail, music always smoothed out the rough spots and made the tedious times seem less so. I remember on our first full-length trail trip, when I was sixteen, we listened to a lot of Beatles and Bob Dylan as well as a fair amount of a band known as The Band, and a singer named Harry Nielsen, whose lyric "You can climb the mountain, You can swim the sea, You can jump into the fire, but you'll never be free" seemed to be our refrain that summer.

I am fortunate to have friends who make wonderful music about the story of Lewis and Clark, and to me it seems the most natural association. Could there ever have been a successful voyage of discovery without those fiddles? Without some tasty treats or games to play? I doubt it. And I know for sure they would not have succeeded without the friendship of the people they met and the people they traveled with. When John Colter decided to head back upriver rather than home to St. Louis, his fellow Corpsmen gave him the items they knew they would not need but that he would require to survive. One Colter biographer writes that these would have included knives, powder horns, hatchets, and other small personal utensils used by a man living in the open. I wonder if someone threw in a mouth harp.

So the next time you are preparing for a road trip, remember to pack your tapes and your fiddles, always plan for some diversions, and don't forget to pack the jerky.

5. Selected and Implanted by Nature
Leadership and Manly Firmness
on the Lewis and Clark Trail

When Thomas Jefferson entrusted Meriwether Lewis with the leadership of the Corps of Northwestern Discovery, he wrote it was because Lewis possessed

> a firmness & perseverance of purpose which nothing but impossibilities could divert from it's direction, . . . careful as a father of those committed to his charge, yet steady in the maintenance of order & discipline . . . of sound understanding and a fidelity to truth so scrupulous that whatever he should report would be as certain as if seen by ourselves, with all of these qualifications as if *selected and implanted by nature* [italics added] in one body, for this express purpose, I could have no hesitation in confiding the enterprize to him.[1]

It appears Jefferson himself would be inclined to follow Lewis to the ends of the earth. As we know, forty or so brave souls did, and all but one came back alive with fantastic stories to tell.

In examining the record of the expedition and what makes Lewis's achievement so memorable, I turned to the former mayor of New York City and recent presidential candidate, Rudy Giuliani, and his book on leadership. For Giuliani leadership comes from preparing relentlessly. It requires studying and learning independently. He mentioned that he loved to read biographies of great men for inspiration. Giuliani feels that a true leader has a sense of justice and accountability. A good practice for a leader is to "underpromise and overdeliver." I came across other insights into leadership from authors James M. Kouzes and Barry Z. Posner, who collaborated on *The Leadership Challenge*, in which they identify key strategies for successful leaders. They feel leaders should be able to model the way, inspire a shared vision, challenge the process, enable others to act, and encourage the hearts of their followers. Most military historians agree that a good company commander needs to have the spirit of fair play, competence, a willingness to share the risks, and a sense of being a father to a family.

But I always come back to our captain's most underrated gift: an acute sense of timing. He knew when to be a Leader with a capital L, but he also knew when to be a co-captain, when to be the father and disciplinarian, and when to be the comrade. From the beginning Lewis displayed the unique talents of a man capable of leading other men. Under Jefferson's guidance, he assembled goods, men, information, medicines, and even "muscatoe curtains" with an eye toward the minutest detail. Included on his list of purchases in Philadelphia were such various and sundry items as 52 lead canisters (which kept the gunpowder dry and could be melted down for bullets when empty), 12 pounds of castile soap, 2 pounds of tea, 45 flannel shirts, 20 frocks, 15 painted knapsacks, 30 gallons of wine, and 36 pairs of stockings. At 50 dozen, he certainly made sure they had enough Rush's Bilious Pills to treat any illness known or unknown.

During this preparation Lewis never shirked his duty, as laid out by President Jefferson, to learn everything he could about surveying and science. Jefferson sent him to Philadelphia to seek counsel and converse with some of the most learned physicians of the day; he expected Lewis to carry a smallpox vaccine into the wilderness and administer it himself. The lengths of Lewis's preparations, combined with his inherent scientific curiosity, no doubt impressed his men. The careful, some might say obsessive, way Lewis observed, collected, and cataloged the flora and fauna along the river proved him to be a well-trained and methodical leader. And while we know they must have respected his facility with a hunting rifle, I have a feeling they were more heartened to know that he would not be getting them lost in the wilderness. The Corps faithfully believed in his courage undaunted. Perhaps the best example of the confidence the men had in Lewis comes from the incident in which Private Windsor almost fell off of the cliff. As Lewis describes it:

I discovered his danger and the trepedation which he was in gave me still further concern for I expected every instant to see him loose his strength and slip off; altho' much allarmed at his situation I disguised my feelings and spoke very calmly to him and assured him that he was in no kind of danger, to take the knife out of his belt behind him and with his wright hand and dig a hole with it in the face of the bank to receive his wright foot which he did and then raised himself to his knees; I then directed him to take off his mockersons and to come forward on his hands and knees holding the knife in one hand and the gun in the other this he happily effected and escaped.[2]

I like to imagine Windsor, at this moment, the "happily effected," wanting to hug Lewis and thank him "most profusely," as they might say.

The good spirits and willingness to "proceed on" without complaint must, in part, be due to the fact that the Corps sensed that they had some say in the outcome of their fate. From court-martials at Wood River and the whippings they dished out, to the Marias or Missouri decisions as to which was the main channel, the men were at each other's mercy. One of the privates told his grandchildren that "lashes well laid on" meant lashes from a gun ramrod rather than from switches. The location of Fort Clatsop was a product of consultation. The ultimate treatment of William Bratton's back injury was the result of the medical opinion of fellow private John Shields.

I know from my personal camping experience that when you have a say, or you think you have a say, you do not complain, which is a motivating factor for consulting the crew.

As part of his sense of timing, Lewis knew when to let his co-captain be his co-leader. It is widely acknowledged that Lewis had insisted on an equal rank for Clark, even after secretary of war Henry Dearborn refused to make it official. Although at times, after the expedition, he claimed sole leadership, we know that Lewis desired the same compensation for Clark as he did for himself. Lewis felt perfectly comfortable walking on the shore and leaving Clark in charge of the command and the mapmaking. He let Clark handle his share of the discipline and gave him credit for being the favorite physician of the Native peoples. The journals show that the two captains consulted on names, routes, routines, and medical treatments and demonstrated their friendship and cohesion at every turn. They set a fine example of the sort of heartfelt friendship among men that inspires devotion in those who observe it.

Lewis, something of a loner, knew not to inflict his bad moods and sour tempers on others. After witnessing the failure of the *Experiment*, his iron boat, Lewis's stoic response, as he related in his journal, was that "having nothing further to do I amused myself fishing and caught a few small fish; they were of the species of the white Chub mentioned below the falls, tho' they are small and few in number."[3]

As a leader Lewis knew when to use his commanding voice in dealing with both the men and the Indians. Despite all of the tangible evidence to the contrary he was able to deliver his harangues on making peace and trading with the Americans without losing points for lack of enthusiasm. Dressed in his elaborate uniform, holding his espontoon, Lewis must have looked and sounded quite authoritative. Add to that the bit of sorcery he could perform with the compass and the air gun, and it is no wonder the Natives were impressed.

But did the message he was delivering ever come through to the deliverer? Lewis did not feel the need to go beyond the assignment and rarely showed any compassion for the people he encountered on the way to the Pacific. At times his disdain is palatable. To be fair, Clark had those moments too, but in Lewis they always seem more pronounced. Examples include Lewis's decision to appropriate a canoe without permission and his deliberate act of defiance when he chose to remove the amulets of Side Hill Calf, a dead Piegan warrior, and leave a peace medal in their place so that they "might be informed who we were."[4] Lewis always seems to be distancing himself from the fact that the Indians were fellow human beings capable of understanding disrespect.

In their book *Primal Leadership*, Daniel Golman, Richard Boyatzis, and Annie McKee assert that the emotions of a leader are contagious throughout an organization. General Eisenhower knew this; he said he learned to confide his fears to his pillow. This would have been especially true with the Corps as they were at times copying directly from the captains' journals. On the return journey Lewis could no longer be bothered with practicing diplomacy and obviously just wanted to get home. He would suffer no insults or impediments at this point. The theft of his beloved dog Seaman caused Lewis great consternation and prompted him to order three men to pursue "the theives, with orders if they made the least resistence or difficulty in surrendering the dog to fire on them."[5]

Can you imagine trying to justify that decision to Thomas Jefferson? Around this time, with his patience mostly gone, Lewis still managed to lead his men, but he also took on unreasonable risks and seemed to fall victim to what could be perceived as his own faulty judgment. We can tell that his confidence is at a high point because he splits his party into smaller and smaller groups. No one seems to question this decision, even though Jefferson explicitly tells Lewis in his instructions

in the loss of yourselves, we should lose also the information you will have acquired. By returning safely with that, you may enable us to renew the essay with better calculated means. To your own discretion therefore must be left the degree of danger you may risk, and the point at which you should decline, only saying we wish you to err on the side of your safety, and to bring back your party safe even if it be with less information.[6]

When we look at the incident at Two Medicine in the context of this remark, it seems like Lewis is doing his best not only to take as much rein as Jefferson would give him, but to prove to himself and the men that his leadership knew no bounds. It seems not even the forty-ninth parallel, the border with Canada, could contain the self-assurance of Meriwether Lewis.

Lewis knew when to be the father figure and when to be the strict disciplinarian. He let the men know that decorum mattered and that mutinous expressions would not be tolerated. When searching for the Shoshone and the herds of horses that would take them over the mountains, Lewis lost his temper because he assumed his men had scared them off: "I now felt quite as much mortification and disappointment as I had pleasure and expectation at the first sight of this indian. I fet soarly chagrined at the conduct of the men particularly Shields to whom I principally attributed this failure in obtaining an introduction to the natives."[7]

We know he loses his temper, because he admits that he "abraids the men a little for their want of attention and imprudence on this occasion." I pity poor Shields and the others when I think of Lewis "abraiding" them right out there in front of God, on the windy high plains, with the Shoshone and their spotted ponies looking on.

At the same time one can find plenty of examples of Lewis's fatherly concern. He was genuinely concerned for the men's venereal complaints and did not hesitate to put modesty aside and extract a vow of celibacy from the injured parties. When the rain at Fort Clatsop seemed never-ending he arranged to have conical hats made for all of the men. And as many times as Shannon got lost, Lewis always sent someone to bring him back. If the men forgot something or let the horses get away, one senses them shrugging, turning back, and saying, "We know what the Captain will say."

Lastly, Lewis knew when to be one of the Corps, when to let his guard down and be just one of the mates. Recall that Lewis once cooked suet dumplings to add to the dinner pot as a well-deserved treat for his comrades. The humorous way he describes Charbonneau preparing the boudin blanc and its final step of baptism in the Missouri with "two dips and a flirt" indicates that he could share a hearty laugh with the men. The evenings around the smoky fire with the grog and the fiddle and the twinkling eyes were the times when Lewis showed himself to be a leader by being a part of the circle. As a lifelong canoeist I appreciate it when Lewis observes that according to his men, he could "pull a tolerable good pole." He could also be a part of their community. I imagine that the men of the expedition would have done anything for Meriwether Lewis. One of the sweeter moments at Fort Clatsop occurred when Joseph Field presented each of the captains with a writing desk for Christmas. No one ordered Field to perform such a kind gesture; he must have done it out of sincere affection.

Even though he was good at sharing his command, throughout the journals we can find examples of Lewis wanting to be the Cook or Columbus figure. He always seems to be way out ahead when important moments or discoveries were expected. He continually found little ways of reminding Clark and the crew that *he* was the man in charge. At the Lolo Hot Springs, for example, he stayed submerged in the hot water a full nine minutes longer than Clark. Then he made sure everyone knew about it by recording the exact times in his journal. Sometimes Lewis seems to be portraying a character in a stage production, and there is no doubt in his own mind that he has the lead role. When an Indian insults him for eating dog, Lewis shows the offender by signs that he would tomahawk him if he "repeated his insolence." At times he seems just on the verge of snapping, of falling over the cliff.

If you study Lewis carefully I think you can accept the notion of his self-destruction. And not to get too deep into his psychology at this point, I nevertheless think he reveals much about himself when he refers to Sacagawea's son as "it": "The child was very wrestless last night; it's jaw and the back of it's neck are much more swolen than they were yesterday tho' his fever has abated considerably. we gave it a doze of creem of tartar and applyed a fresh poultice of onions."[8]

From a man who referred to boats as "she" and to grizzly bears as "gentlemen," this is a bit hard to swallow. At Three Forks, where Sacagawea had been captured and taken by the Hidatsa, he noted on July 28, 1805, "Indian woman was one of the female prisoners taken at that time; tho' I cannot discover that she shews any immotion of sorrow in recollecting this event or of joy in being again restored to her native country; if she has enough to eat and a few trinkets to wear I believe she would be perfectly content anywhere."

And Lewis seems incapable of acknowledging her emotional reaction to seeing her brother Cameahwait again. Because he was afraid of being perceived as weak, Lewis would never admit that he cried for sentimental reasons. He could not admit that he cared for a Native's child and shared a common bond of humanity with him. Clark admitted it. Lewis never did. The weight of Jefferson's expectations, the reality of being an administrator, facing a deadline, insolvency, chemical dependencies, his basic psychological makeup, and the lack of a significant other all contributed to Lewis's demise. But I believe it was his essential inability to admit that he was just like the rest of us that finally brought him down.

In doing the research for the book *The Lewis and Clark Companion* and in studying Jackson's *Letters* I came across an insightful quote from the artist Charles Willson Peale. He was writing to his son about Clark and his decision to use an editor for the publication of the journals: "I found that the General was too diffident of his abilities. I would rather see a single narrative with such observations as I am sure Clark could have made on the different Nations of Savages & things, which the Notes taken by Capt. Lewis would have passed over unnoticed."[9]

Clark's letter to Charbonneau, in which he offers to educate his son in St. Louis and to help Charbonneau find a job, reveals that he knew that the lack of compensation for Sacagawea's interpretive services was an injustice. When it became obvious that he was the only person who could ensure the publication of the journals, Clark stepped forward even though he doubted his own abilities. Getting the job done seemed to be his forte.

Is Clark the better human being, or perhaps just the one less preoccupied with being a hero? I think Clark was content to be mortal, and as we know from his treatment of York and some of his questionable dealings with tribes east of the Mississippi, he was capable of regret. Lewis never seemed to want to acknowledge his mortality or that he could possibly be flawed or regret any of his actions. When he returned it was "his late tour"; altogether his expedition, but in the end he knew that it would be only Clark coming to his rescue. One tenet of leadership is the ability to lead his own life. Another one is that "the fire of a truly great leader is always burning." Somehow when Captain Lewis returned from his rendezvous with destiny his fire went out. I respect and admire Meriwether Lewis, and I believe his men held him in genuine affection, but it is Clark who knew how to lead his own life, how to keep the fire burning. If I may be so bold, I would say that Jefferson got it a bit wrong when he wrote that Lewis's qualifications as a good leader were "as if selected and implanted by nature" in *one* body. The reality was two bodies: Lewis's *and* Clark's. Perhaps the Corps understood this best. Alexander Willard fathered seven sons and named one in honor of his Captain Lewis and another in honor of his Captain Clark.

6. Sufficiently Ample

What If?

I think more study should be given to the "what ifs" of Lewis and Clark, including some of their near pitfalls and "minor" oversights.

A few years ago at the Lewis and Clark Trail Heritage Foundation annual meeting, President Ron Laycock argued that Lewis and Clark's biggest mistake was their failure to hire Pierre Dorion as interpreter for the councils with the Teton Sioux. Historian Paul Cutright states that packing thermometers might have been a mistake, since all were broken before the party crossed the Rockies. The lack of tobacco by the end of March forced the men to grind and smoke their pipes (which had tobacco flavor) and red willow bark for enjoyment. The "what if" scenario is frequently applied to the trading vessels that were supposed to resupply the Corps; to the lack of an artist or a certified doctor; and, of course, to the iron boat. Some folks laugh at archeologist Ken Karsminski's opinion that finding the remnants of the iron boat would be the equivalent of finding the Holy

Grail. But when you realize that someone recently paid $115,000 at auction for a Jefferson peace medal, Karsminski's assertion does not sound so far-fetched.

On the subject of "what ifs" I thought of one mistake that might seem a small oversight on Lewis's part but which could ultimately have cost the expedition members their lives. I do not mean their daily ration of grog (another thing Lewis could have packed more of). I am speaking of that little trifle, the blue bead. Among the twenty-three hundred pounds of supplies and equipment Lewis assembled in Philadelphia were presents for Indians consisting of items such as shirts, handkerchiefs, looking glasses, needles, scissors, thimbles, thread, vermillion, knives, tomahawks, fishing awls, combs, blankets, tobacco, ribbons, kettles, and 432 curtain rings "sufficiently large for the Finger." In addition Lewis carried wampum, or white shell-like beads, which, while highly valued among northeastern tribes and regarded as currency there, had little value once he reached the Pacific Coast. In fact they brought some wampum back with them to St. Louis.

Before I proceed let me say that after years of car and boat camping I appreciate a good packer, and I think Lewis, for the most part, was one. He certainly brought enough ink, gunpowder, and peace medals to last the duration of the trip. Along their route they distributed some eighty-six medals in three sizes. The medals would have been familiar to some Natives and valued as an acknowledgement of their sovereign nation status, but other Natives were not quite sure what to make of them. Author Thomas Slaughter points out that one Cheyenne chief was "alarmed" by the symbol on the medal, which showed two men shaking hands, an unfamiliar and apparently somewhat threatening gesture for the Cheyenne. Efforts are underway today to inventory the remaining peace medals, and a member of the Walla Walla tribe, Ron Pond, is working on his doctoral dissertation on peace medals at Washington State University.

I think we also need a dissertation on blue beads. Lewis bought thirty-three pounds of assorted beads in May and June 1803 from Philadelphia merchants Christian Denchla and Jonathan and Charles Wister, amounting to 11 percent of his total $669.50 expenditure on presents for Indians. Bead expert Gene Mouw says that the beads would measure out at roughly a hundred fathoms at ten per string. They were opaque, light blue glass beads from China and were most likely identical to the padre beads of the American Southwest, having arrived into the Northwest by way of Alaska with Vitus Bering and the Russians. They were not the cylindrical black-and-white beads, sometimes called Lewis and Clark beads, which came decades later.

In assembling the presents, Lewis followed the plan of President Jefferson and the advice of the War Department and its secretary, Henry Dearborn, whose Indian policy centered on the idea of establishing Indian trading posts where fur pelts could be traded for the U.S. Government Supply House's manufactured goods. Jefferson imagined that this would foster dependence among the tribes, who then could easily be persuaded to give up their landholdings and become yeoman farmers. Peace would prevail because the United States would pay a fixed price for the fur; the Indians would not be subject to price variations as they were with the fur trade companies. The Indians' dependence would be complete and was obviously essential to the plan.

In gathering the presents, purveyor of public supplies Israel Wheelan followed the method already established by the fur companies and the interests of Russian, Spanish, and English explorers in the upper Missouri and coastal regions: present medals, flags, and presents, though perhaps not curtain rings, to individuals of influence within the tribes. Lewis also probably obtained information on presents from Pierre and Auguste Chouteau as well as from Manuel Lisa. The goods were carefully parceled up with the help of John Hay, a postmaster and North

West Company trader of Cahokia, Illinois, into fourteen bales and one box so they could be distributed and unpacked one by one along the way to the Pacific. On June 19, 1803, when Lewis wrote to Clark inviting him to be his co-captain and telling him he should be "extremely happy in his company," he also assured him that "my supply of Indian presents is sufficiently ample."[1] Or so he hoped.

From the list of requirements Lewis submitted, he noted of the blue bead, "This is a coarse cheap bead imported from China & costing in England 13 d. the lbs. in strands. It is far more valued than the white beads of the same manufacture and answers all the purposes of money, being counted by the fathom."[2]

He knew they were more valuable and they were certainly cheap. What prevented him from purchasing more? Why did they assume the rate of exchange would be set by the interloper and not the residents? What made the Americans think they could impose their value systems on the tribes that lived along the Missouri and Columbia rivers? And when the Clatsop proved "great higglers in trade," as Lewis called them, why did the captains take it as an insult? Was it because they realized Jefferson's whole concept of convincing the Indians to trade with the Americans for American goods exclusively was a pipe dream? Archeologist Colleen Hamilton states that at this time, "The merchandise offered to the natives in trade had to be suited to their tastes. Beads were sought by men and women alike and were used for personal adornment, for ceremonial functions and communication devices."

For some tribes the color blue represented the spirit world; add that fact to the notion that the Indians wanted quality goods and knew that the U.S. Government Supply Houses offered lesser merchandise, especially blankets, and we see that the problem was the sophistication of tribal tastes and the inability of the Americans to appreciate the connection between the bead and any sort of spiritual meaning. The Indians knew who held all the cards in the situation on the Pacific Coast during the winter of 1805–6. The Natives were not the ones whining about the weather and the lack of food. The Americans were trying to impose their value system at a time when what they really needed was "sufficiently ample" supplies of a seemingly worthless item, suddenly literally worth its weight in gold. So long as the United States offered insufficient or inferior trade items, Jefferson's vision of an empire of liberty seemed to be in jeopardy.

During early trading episodes with the Clatsop, Clark noted on November 22, 1805, that in hopes of obtaining a sea otter skin, he offered "my Watch, handkerchief a bunch of red beads and a dollar of the American Coin, all of which he refused and demanded ti a co mo shack which is Chief Beads and the most common blue beads, but fiew of which we happen to have at this time."

The winter before, Lewis acknowledged in his "Fort Mandan Miscellany" that "the nations in every quarter I am told are fond of blue beads, red paint, knives, axes, Guns and ammunition." During the winter at Fort Mandan, perhaps John Shields should have been selling his smithing services for blue beads *and* food, not strictly for food.

On December 12, 1805, at Fort Clatsop, Clark recorded of the Clatsop Indians, "I can readily discover that they are Close deelers & Stickle for verry little, never close a bargain except they think they have the advantage Value Blue beeds highly, white they also prise but no other Colour do they Value in the least."

What would it have meant if they did indeed have "sufficiently ample" supplies of blue beads? It would have had vast repercussions on the way they related to the Natives on the Columbia plateau and Pacific Coast. Perhaps their observations would all have been positive ones: "Yes these savages helped us and supplied all of the dogs, berries, fish and roots we needed just for a basketful of the blue beed." Instead, one week later, on December 20, 1805, Clark complains,

> 3 Indians arrive in a Canoe. they brought with them mats, roots &Sackacome berries to Sell for which they asked Such high prices that we did not purchase any of them. Those people ask generally double and tribble the value of what they have to Sell and never take less than the real value of the article in Such things as is calculated to do them Service. Such as Blue & white beeds with which they trade with the nativs above . . . Tobacco and blue beeds they do prefur to everything.

The high price Clark writes about must be considered a relative thing. If they had carried an ample supply of blue beads, living conditions that winter on the coast would likely not have been so miserable.

Lewis describes the power of the blue bead best on January 9, 1806: "The natives are extravegantly fond of the most common cheap blue and white beads, of moderate size, or such that from 50 to 70 will weigh on penneywieght. [1/20th of a troy ounce, according to Gary Moulton] the blue is usually preferred to the white; these beads constitute the principal circulating medium with all the indian tribes on this river; for these beads they will dispose of any article they possess."

In his *History of the Lewis and Clark Expedition* Lewis and Clark scholar Elliot Coues adds, "Indeed if the example of civilized life did not completely vindicate their choice, we might wonder at their infatuated attachment to a bauble in itself so worthless. Yet these beads are quite as reasonable objects of research as the precious metals, and the great circulating medium of trade with all the nations on the Columbia."[3]

Perhaps if Jefferson and Lewis had been less cocksure of their diplomacy they would have brought more of what the Natives really wanted, not what the Americans expected them to value. Lewis would have been able to purchase as many sea otter robes as he desired if he could have appreciated that, for the Natives, blue beads had more than an ornamental value. They were symbols not only of power and wealth but also of a spiritual connection and were vastly more important than Lewis and Jefferson understood.

On January 19, 1806, the Captains purchased a sea otter robe with the last of their blue beads "consisting of six fathoms." Recall they started the trip with a hundred fathoms. On February 15, 1806, Lewis noted that a good horse could be purchased from the Natives for "a few beads or other paltry trinkets which in the U states would not cost more than one or two dollars. This abundance and cheapness of horses will be advantageous to those who may hereafter attempt the fir trade to the East Indies by way of the Columbia River and the Pacific Ocean."

But for Lewis and his party the old adage "If wishes were horses, beggars would ride" seems particularly applicable here. On March 11, 1806, when they were able to scrounge up some food, Lewis declares that "we once more live in clover; Anchovies fresh Sturgeon and Wappetoe." Nevertheless he realistically summed up their worldly possessions:

two handkerchiefs would now contain all the small articles of merchandize which we possess; the ballance of the stock consists of 6 blue robes one scarlet do. one uniform artillerist's coat and hat, five robes made of our large flag, and a few our old cloaths trimed with ribbon. on this stock we have wholy to depend for the purchase of horses and such portion of our subsistence form the Indians as it will be in our power to obtain. a scant dependence indeed for the tour of the distance of that before us.

If he had packed enough beads they never would have left "the clover," and the incident of canoe theft could have been avoided. On March 20, 1806, as they were preparing to leave Fort Clatsop, Lewis lamented, "It would have been very fortunate for us had some of those traders arrived previous to our departure from hence; as we should then have had it in our power to abtain an addition to our stock of merchandize, which would have made our homeward bound journey much more comfortable."

At one point in February the party's stock of food was reduced to less than one day's worth, and that was mostly rotten elk meat. The Corps departed from Fort Clatsop on March 23, 1806, earlier than they had planned simply because they had nothing left to eat.

On April 20, Captain Lewis wrote, "I barted my Elk skins old irons and 2 canoes for beads. one of the canoes for which they would give us but little I had cut up for fuel."

That Lewis was losing his patience is understandable, but I wonder if he wasn't a little annoyed with himself as well.

By April 24, when the Natives realized the Americans would no longer need their canoes, they refused to offer anything to trade for them. Lewis reacted with an order to Drouillard to begin chopping up the boats. The Indians countered with an offer to purchase them for several strands of beads. Lewis accepted. The beads helped the party trade for supplies on the return trip; they were vital in sustaining the Corps, and of much greater value than the captain and his advisors previously realized. On May 13, 1806, with the Nez Perce, Lewis again remarks on the blue beads' value: "They do not appear to be so much devoted to baubles as most of the nations we have met with, but seem anxious always to obtain articles of utility, such as knives, axes, tommahawks, kettles blankets and mockerson alls. blue beads however may form an exception to this remark; this article among all nations of this country may be justly compared to goald or silver among civlized nations."

Also in May, on the Kooskooskee River with the Nez Perce, the captains resorted to medical quackery to feed the troops. The situation was so dire by June 22 that the captains were likely overjoyed to give Whitehouse a few beads that Captain Clark "had unexpectedly found in one of his waistcoat pockets" to purchase a salmon for the hungry crew.

On June 2 the captains were forced to use their officer coats' buttons of silver and gold. If Lewis had packed enough blue beads he could have worn his officer's coat upon arriving back in St. Louis; who knows what that could have done for his self-esteem.

A fortnight earlier, on May 20 at Camp Chopunnish, Lewis described the destitution faced by his men: "Brass buttons is an article of which these people are tolerably fond, the men have taken advantage of their prepossession in favour of buttons and have devested themselves of all they had in possesson which they had given in exchange for roots and bread."

One day later, in light of their situation

we divided the remnant of our store of merchandize among our party with a view that each should purchase therewith a parsel of roots and bread from the natives as his stores for the rocky mountains for there seems but little probability that we shall be enabled to make any dryed meat for that purpose and we cannot as yet form any just idea what resource the fish will furnish us. Each man's stock in trade amounts to no more than one awl, one Kniting pin, a half an ounce of vermillion, two nedles, a few scanes of thread and about a yard of ribbon; a slender stock indeed with which to lay in a store of provision for that dreary wilderness.

As Coues notes in his *History of the Lewis and Clark Expedition*, the Corps did not lack credit. "They were furnished by President

Jefferson with probably the most compressive letter of credit ever handed to any individuals. What was lacking at the mouth of the Columbia was simply a stock of kickshaws and trumpery for Clatsop barter."[4]

According to the *Oxford English Dictionary*, a kickshaw is "something uncommon or something that has no particular name," and trumpery is showy but worthless finery. Sounds like an apt description of a beaver skin hat. Ultimately it seems Lewis felt the same way, as Jefferson wrote to Secretary Dearborn in February 1807 about blue beads, "He says that were his journey to be performed again, one half or ⅔ of his stores in value should be of these."[5]

What else can we say about the blue beads? Perhaps they sealed the deal on the August 13, when Lewis desperately needed Shoshone horses to get over the Bitterroot. At the crucial moment, according to Lewis, "after Smoking a few pipes with them I distributed some trifles among them, with which they seemed much pleased particularly with the blue beads and the vermillion."

And what about November 20, 1805, when the captains took Sacagawea's belt of blue beads so that they could trade it for a sea otter robe that Clark declared was more "butifull" than any robe he had ever seen? "Both Captain Lewis and my Self endeavored to purchase the roab with differant articles at length we precured it for a belt of blue beeds which the Squar—wife of our interpreter Shabono wore around her waste."

Did they ever appropriate personal property from the rest of the Corps? How did they "precure" Sacagawea's belt? Did they wait until she was asleep and have Charbonneau steal it in the night? I wonder if the guilt was too much for them, especially Clark, who notes the next day that they gave her a coat of blue cloth in exchange. I asked Amy Mossett, Hidatsa member and authority on Sacagawea, about that belt, and she theorizes it came from Charbonneau and was not, as I had understood, a gift given to her by other women for being a hard worker. According to Amy, all of the women worked hard. Sacagawea would not have been unique in that regard. If marriage to the Frenchman afforded status symbols like the blue-beaded belt perhaps her marriage to him was not such a bad thing after all.

While it is obvious that I am no expert, I find the subject of blue beads endlessly fascinating. Once on the Missouri River Breaks I watched longtime outfitter Larry Cook pull a blue bead out of an anthill. He explained to me that you sometimes find beads that way at the top of the anthill where the ants have pushed out the deepest part of their mound. Now when I hike in the hills around the Missouri I always search the tops of anthills for that elusive blue bead, one Lewis could have used on the Columbia.

7. Opening Our Ears

Researching *The Lewis and Clark Companion*

When President Thomas Jefferson sent Lewis and Clark out to follow the Missouri River to its source and find their way to the Pacific Ocean, he first instructed Lewis in June 1803, "In all your intercourse with the natives, treat them in the most friendly and conciliatory manner which their own conduct will admit; allay all jealousies as to the object of your journey, satisfy them of its innocence, make them acquainted with the position, extent, character, peaceable and commercial dispositions of the U.S., of our wish to be neighborly, friendly and useful to them."[1]

In order to implement these instructions they would need to, as historian James Ronda points out, "tread carefully," or in the vernacular spoken by both parties, keep their ears open and not listen to what they sometimes called "the crowing of Bad Birds."

As we study the journals and the writings about the expedition it becomes clear that in certain circumstances the men of the Corps of Discovery did have their ears open, especially when respect for their hosts was at its peak, as with the Mandan and Nez Perce. They did appreciate Native sensibilities on some occasions. When it came to the practical and the temporal, the Corps was listening. On other occasions, however, their hearing seems to have been blocked. They were not able to come to terms with or hear the Indians when it came to the Native emphasis on spirits, "medicine," and the transference of that medicine from one culture to another. Their prejudices, combined with President Jefferson's limited understanding of Indian beliefs and established trading systems, sparked a misunderstanding that is still with us today. Part of the reason for compiling *The Lewis and Clark Companion* was that Clay Jenkinson and I wanted to come to an understanding of what they missed, what they overlooked, and what they did not hear.

While working on the *Companion* we paid attention to the people who provided a sharper focus to Native sensibilities. We referred to firsthand accounts along with reference guides and encyclopedias that described individual Indians as historic figures remarkable in their own right. These sources contained accounts delineating Indian tribes as distinct nations that were as different from each other as white cultures were from them. We tried to shed light on some of the people who called the northern plains and coastal regions home. After years of lying dormant in the landscape of the story of the expedition, we tried to pull them out, wake them up, and share them with an ever-growing audience of interested readers of Lewis and Clark scholarship.

The reader can see how the complicated relationship between the two cultures led to a series of misunderstandings and how the overriding prejudices of the Virginia and Kentucky army officers, sons of the American Revolution, affected every single interchange between themselves and the Natives. If you read the journals you know that early in the journey one wise Arikara leader asked Lewis and Clark why their "father" would present the Indians with liquor that would make them fools. The captains noted the question but were too busy following orders to realize its ramifications for future diplomatic efforts. They did not hear the underlying question: How can we trust you when we see you are so willing to lower us from men to fools just so that you can laugh at us?

Part of Jefferson's mandate for Lewis and Clark was to send back tribal members to visit and negotiate with himself and secretary of war Henry Dearborn. Lewis sent a delegation of chiefs of the Osage, Missouri, Kansas, Oto, Pani, Iowa, and Sioux tribes. During this visit, in January 1806, Jefferson naively promised the delegation, "In establishing a trade with you we desire to make no profit. We shall ask from you only what everything costs us, and give you for your furs and pelts whatever we can get from them again. Be assured you shall find advantage in this change of your friends."

His intentions were good but his understanding of the intricacies of tribal trading patterns already established on the northern Great Plains was lacking. In their answer to the president, the delegation foreshadowed the tone of American Indian relations with the U.S. government for many years to come. Not only were they skeptical about the ability of a distant federal government to control individual actions, they doubted white promises to effect a positive change.

Fathers: you say that you are as numerous as the stars in the skies, & as strong as numerous. So much the better, fathers, tho', if you are so, we will see you ere long punishing all the wicked Red skins that you'll find amongst us, & you may tell to your white Children on our lands, to follow your orders, & to not do as they please, for they do not keep your word. Our Brothers who Came here before told us you had ordered good things to be done & sent to our villages, but we have seen nothing, & your waged Men think that truth will not reach your ears, but we are Conscious that we must speak the truth, truth must be spoken to the ears of our fathers, and our fathers must open their ears for the truth to get in.[2]

One aspect of the complexities of the interchanges between the U.S. government representatives and the Native populations can be glimpsed in the story of Sheheke-shote, the Mandan chief known as White Coyote who agreed to return with the expedition in 1806 and go to Washington to meet with the "Great Father." Sheheke journeyed with his wife, Yellow Corn, and their children, along with his translator, Rene Jessuame, and his family to St. Louis, Charlottesville, and eventually to Washington. Although his return was hampered by several incidents related to intertribal warfare, he finally arrived back in his homeland in 1809. He remained a respected chief of his people until he died as a consequence of the War of 1812.

In the course of researching the *Companion*, we learned something interesting about the Shoshone guide Toby, sometimes called Old Toby, who was hired by the captains at Cameahwait's suggestion. Professor John Rees, in a 1958 article in *Idaho Yesteryears*, quotes a trader who lived among the Lemhi Shoshone in the late 1800s as saying that the Shoshone name that Toby was known by among the Corps, Divo koo'vishe, meant "Furnishes White Man with Brains." But this was not his only name. His "real" name, Pi'hey'keen Quee'yah', meant "Swooping Eagle" because of his reputation as a fierce fighter. Similarly, Sacagawea's brother's name Cameahwait meant "Not Inclined to Go" or "He Who Never Walks," but his "real" name, Too'aid Coo'tee', meant "Fires the Black Gun." Rees explains that the whites viewed names differently from the Natives. The Shoshone were hesitant to reveal their "real," or secret, names because that meant revealing something that could lessen their power or expose them to danger in some way. A stranger would have to earn the privilege of hearing these names. In public and on various occasions they used other names. These might originate at the spur of the moment and could be related to an incident occurring at a given time. Hence Toby called himself "Furnishes White Man with Bruins" because that was how he saw his role among the Corps.

The *Companion* contains entries on several artists associated with Lewis and Clark and their Native contacts. In a long list of characters some men stand out, such as George Catlin. Catlin's fascination with Native peoples led him up the Missouri in 1832, and his art is closely associated with the expedition because he painted some of the same people the captains mention in their journals. His talent was viewed with awe by the Mandan, who believed he could capture a person's spirit by painting a portrait of them. One young girl, whose name means "The Mink," whom he had painted and persuaded to allow him to keep her portrait, became violently ill when he started back down the river with her image. Her relatives sent a messenger who told him, "She is dying, the picture you made of her is too much like her—you put so much of her into it, that when your boat took it away from our village, it drew part of her life with it—she is bleeding from the mouth—she is puking up all her blood—you are drawing the strings out of her heart and they will soon break. We must take her picture back and then she will get well again."[3]

Catlin heard and understood this request. He reluctantly agreed to return the portrait but learned later that she died anyway. No doubt because of this experience and others like it, Catlin came to realize and respect the Indian regard for the concept of spirit and how it encompassed every single element of their lives.

We tried to explore and explain what Natives meant by "medicine" as opposed to what the Corps meant by it. Whenever they felt it would help relations or improve symptoms, the captains used their medicine or science. By treating Natives with an eye wash or eye water, the captains found that they could exchange their services for things they needed. They recognized that even though they were not curing the people, they were alleviating their symptoms. As long as they were not consciously hurting their patients Lewis and Clark justified the treatments and continued to administer them as long as they could or needed to.

Following Jefferson's instructions they collected plants and described the medicinal applications as used by the Natives. Trader Hugh Heney gave Lewis the top of a purple coneflower plant (echinacea) that he said the Natives used to "cure (the bite) of mad Dogs Snakes &c," and explained that the patient should apply the plant to the bitten part twice a day, adding that "the bitten person is not to chaw or Swallow any of the Root for it might have contrary effect."

While following Jefferson's instructions and collecting the cures of the tribes, the captains failed to appreciate that for Natives, the meaning of "medicine" was much more complex. For European Americans, medicine involved strictly scientific applications. For Indians, medicine, as Lewis interpreted their definition, meant "that in which the power of God is manifest by its incomprehensible power of action." So, for example, Sergeant Gass could comment on the "superstitious credulity" of the Mandan when they presented food to a buffalo skull with the belief that it would hasten the arrival of the buffalo. For whites medicine involved science and reason; for Indians it involved the spirit of divine energy that they could access through ceremony and ritual.

One example, found in the journals, is the night a Nez Perce woman was "possessed" by her *wyakin*, or guardian spirit. An explanation for this behavior came much later, in 1979, from Nez Perce historian Alvin Josephy, who wrote, "The Wyakin belief reflected a Nez Perce universe filled with individual spirits that existed in dreams and in real life, and to which the Nez Perce could appeal for assistance: Thunder, lightning, a soaring eagle, a grizzly bear, and so forth. Each spirit could harm or protect a man according to its powers and inclination. Each man (or woman) had a personal Wyakin warning him, protecting him, and assisting him through his life on earth."[4]

This notion seemed foreign and strange to Ordway and Clark, but to the people of the woman's tribe it was not such an unusual occurrence and could be incorporated into what they saw as their medicine, in much the same way as Catholics would acknowledge someone making the sign of the cross on the breast as acceptable to their worldview. In the *Companion* we cite a concept related by Morris Berman, a historian of ideas, that the expedition carried a "disenchanted mindset" into a world that was seen by the Indians as fully alive with spirit.

An example of this sort of medicine can be seen in the gruesome end of interpreter George Drouillard's life. After the expedition, Drouillard (part Shawnee, part French, and sign talker for the Corps) returned to the headwaters of the Missouri to trap beaver. Despite the threatening presence of the nearby Blackfeet, Drouillard kept going out to set his traps. He said he was too much of an Indian to be caught off guard by other Indians.[5] When the Blackfeet warriors found him out by himself, they attacked him and finally killed him after a hard-fought battle during which Drouillard distinguished himself through his bravery and refusal to give up. The warriors then decided to eat him—according to the journals of Alexander Henry the Younger, "parts raw and parts boiled"—probably so they could capture some of his spirit, bravery, and "medicine" for themselves.

Along with sharing forms of entertainment like music, dancing, and playing games, sharing food was another important way of exchanging and listening to each other. The Corps learned how the Natives gathered wild roots like the cous, camas, and wappato. They tasted them and ate traditional Native foods such as bitterroot, breadroot, euchalon, Jerusalem artichokes, ground beans, and pemmican. Except for Clark, they acquired a taste for dog. The Corps discovered that while some tribes raised dogs for meat, others, like the Shoshone, refused to eat dog meat because of its similarity to one of their holy creatures, the coyote. They also learned that to some tribes, the idea of eating horseflesh was repulsive.

Lewis appreciated the eucholon, or anchovy, as prepared by the Indians:

I find them best when cooked Indian stile, which is by roasting a number of them together on a wooden spit without any previous preparation whatsoever. They are so fat they require no additional sauce, and I think them superior to any fish I ever tasted even more delicate and lussious than the white fish of the lakes which heretofore forme my standart of excellence among fishes. I have heard the fresh anchovy much extolled but I hope I shall be pardoned for believing this quite as good. (February 24, 1806)

Regarding shelter, Lewis came to enjoy sleeping on buffalo robes so much that when he returned to civilization, he could not sleep in a bed; he preferred to lie on his robes on the ground. During the expedition, the captains shared what they called the "leather lodge," or tipi, of Charbonneau, Sacagawea, and their child when they were on the river, and continued to use it until May 1806 when it wore out. When he was paid, Charbonneau received extra pay for his lodge, as it had been put to "public use." It is hard to imagine the U.S. government paying rent on a tipi. One of the lesser-known discoveries or lessons of the expedition was the wide variety of shelter used among the different tribes. During their travels the Corps came across earth lodges, mat houses, shelters made from rushes, and cedar plank houses, among others.

The Corps adopted Native styles of clothing to suit their needs. They took to moccasin making, fashioning 358 pairs during the winter at Fort Clatsop. Lewis and Clark admired the coastal sea otter robe; they appropriated Sacagawea's blue bead belt from her so they could purchase one. They also favored the conical hats worn by the Clatsop Indians and measured their heads and ordered one for each member of the party during the rainy winter on the Pacific Coast. Lewis took such pride in the tippet given to him by Cameahwait that in 1807 he posed wearing it in a painting by St. Memin. The journals note many traditional items of trade, such as blue beads, dentalium, ermine tails, euchalon oil, sea otter, and other pelts. Lewis also recognized the superior craftsmanship of the bows made by Natives from bighorn sheep horns and the market potential in combs made from these horns, writing on May 25, 1806, "I have no doubt but it would be eligant and ucefull hair combs, and might probably answer as many valuable purposes to civilized man, as it dose to the savages, who form their watercups spoons and platters of it."

Notice Lewis's language here. When we think of water cups, spoons, and platters, we do not usually associate the word "savage" with such sophisticated tableware.

Several times the party had to acknowledge that their hosts had superior methods of manufacture or animal husbandry. For example, the captains admitted that the Nez Perce method of gelding horses was superior to their own in that the wounds healed more quickly and tended not to bleed as much. They also adopted the Nez Perce way of burning out, rather than hacking out, trees for a canoe, because it was less labor-intensive. Some things puzzled the Corps: Why would the Mandan dismantle a perfectly good corn mill that the captains gave them in the winter of 1804–5? The explanation is simple: they wanted to use the iron parts for their weapons and hide-scraping tools, and they already had their own perfectly suitable way of grinding corn.

On the Columbia River, the expedition's carpenter, Sergeant Patrick Gass, noted on March 30, 1806, "the natives of this country ought to have the credit of making the finest canoes, perhaps in the world, both as to service and beauty; and are no less expert in working them when made."

Many times it seems the Corps was in too much of a hurry to listen carefully. Although they did take the time to record elements of Indian beliefs or religion, many times the captains dismissed these beliefs as mere superstition. As readers we wish they had taken adequate time or given more credence to the ceremonies and traditions involving sacred animals, like the buffalo calling dance, or the Nez Perce first salmon of the season ceremony. As Lewis wrote on April 19, 1806, at Celilo Falls, "There was great joy with the natives last night in consequence of the arrival of the salmon; one of those fish was caught; this was the harbinger of good news to them. They informed us that those fish would arrive in great quantities in the course of about 5 days. This fish was dressed and being divided into small pieces was given to each child in the village. This custom is founded in the superstitious opinion that it will hasten the arrival of the salmon."

As authors Dan Landeen and Allen Pinkham point out, the Nez Perce believed that if they performed the ceremony correctly a good fishing season would result. They believed they were related to the salmon, and that their deceased relations were, in fact, the salmon. Lewis and Clark had no way of understanding this or of placing it into any other context than "superstition."

The men on the Lewis and Clark Expedition did not hear the corn-singing songs of the Arikara women, likely because they were with the Arikara at the wrong time of the year, but also because as visitors they assumed the women were drudges, not controllers of the means of wealth for the whole community. They certainly would not have understood that for the women, planting crops was regarded as highly and as much a part of their being as giving birth. They sang to the corn like they sang to their own children. The Corps did not see the offerings Shoshone women would make to mice in exchange for harvesting ground beans from their nut stashes and likely would not have understood such an offering made to the mice they recognized as relatives, not vermin. To understand the importance of these symbols and beliefs, you have to do your own digging. You must examine accounts from Native sources, which explains why these beliefs retained validity in the past, and continue to do so to this day.

For instance, if we look at the buffalo calling dance simply from the eyes of the explorers in the early 1800s we see only part of the picture. The men were glad to take part in a ceremony that for them was all about the strangers being "big medicine" that would be transferred to their hunters if the Corps slept with their wives. Granted, if you read the journals and look at Catlin's paintings of these strange dances, they are an intriguing part, but it remains only one ingredient to the overall meal. Authors such as Virginia Roberts Peters and her book *Women of the Earth Lodges* help us understand that offering young women to visitors or older members of the tribe as bed partners was a complicated tradition, and one that involved the women not just as "pipelines to power" as James Ronda calls them, but as sources of power in their own right. Ronda sees the buffalo calling dance as a transmittal ceremony, but for many of the women it meant a step up in status among their clans and one in which they themselves played a crucial and active part.

One way to open your ears is to open your mind and see yourself as a part of nature, not removed from it. When the tribes acknowledged that connection through the buffalo calling dance or the first salmon ceremony, the European Americans did not understand that connection. They always viewed themselves as apart from nature, as separate or even above it all. Indigenous peoples tended to see their place in the world as of the same value as the tiniest creature.

Part of the fun of compiling the *Companion* was the friendships and acquaintances struck up along the way. One such friendship is with Amy Mossett of the Three Affiliated Tribes. She helped me to understand things I probably would have never have considered except for her insight. For example, she recently spoke at a conference about the damage done to her culture by the building of the Garrison Dam in 1953. The dam caused the further disintegration of her people because it separated so many of them from each other. In speaking with her later she told me of a centuries-old prophecy that said when the Missouri River flowed backward it signaled the end of the world. In many ways, for the tribes this is in danger of coming true. The river meant life to these people; it was the center of their creation stories, not just a means of transportation or a source of food. But Amy and the rest of the tribes along the river are not surrendering. They are more determined than ever to proceed on and tell the stories of their ancestors' encounter with the expedition and white culture to anyone who will listen.

I think we have finally gotten to a place where our ears are open, or at least semiunplugged, and we are not as much distracted by the crowing of bad birds. We are at a point in our history where we can see the connectedness of humans and nature. We know the impact humans make on their environment. The story of Lewis and Clark and the people they encountered becomes much richer and more enlightening if we remember that there is more than one way of telling and hearing a story.

8. I Grew Heartily Tired of the National Hug

Meriwether Lewis under the Microscope

Fresh from his triumphant return from the land beyond the Louisiana Purchase, Meriwether Lewis faced his own personal and seemingly insurmountable problems. Ill-suited for his position as governor of the Territory of Upper Louisiana he teetered on financial insolvency, his health was deteriorating both physically and mentally, and he had yet to commence writing his journals for publication. His life was spiraling out of control, and he had few friends to offer the good counsel he needed to get over the hump of wondering "What will I do next?" For the first time in his life Meriwether Lewis was lost. The night he stumbled into Grinder's Stand he sorely needed a good friend.

In investigating the reasons behind the untimely death of Meriwether Lewis a handful of explanations emerge. Thomas Jefferson himself posited some of them, calling Lewis "much afflicted with hypochondria" and writing in 1813 that while they lived together in Washington, Lewis exhibited "sensible depressions of the mind." It is natural for students of the expedition to wonder why Lewis left this "sublunary world," as he once called it, in such a disturbing way.

Recovering alcoholics tell me that Lewis was a classic alcoholic. Depressives say he surely was one of them. Bipolar disorder, brain syphilis, and malaria have also been suggested, but none of these present-day diagnoses comes as close, I believe, to revealing his strikingly complex personality as does the recently defined Asperger's syndrome, a highly functioning autistic spectrum disorder, or ASD, that is just beginning to be understood in the scientific community.

When examined one by one, some of Lewis's behaviors appear simply quirky or idiosyncratic. However, when studied in terms of patterns it becomes apparent that Captain Lewis experienced more than just a collection of quirks, all or most of which are symptomatic of people suffering from what we know today as Asperger's. A particular psychological reason may explain why Meriwether Lewis was the way he was. Proceed on with caution: we will never know for sure why Lewis killed himself, just as we will never be positively certain what killed Sergeant Floyd. What follows is pure conjecture, though it is conjecture based on a reading of the facts.[1]

While proceeding on with the Lewis and Clark Expedition Meriwether Lewis was doing what he loved best. This, according to Thomas Jefferson, was "to ramble," taking in every detail "with a fidelity to truth so scrupulous that whatever he should report would be as certain as if seen by ourselves," as Jefferson wrote. In his biographical sketch of Lewis, Jefferson writes of the eight-year-old Meriwether hunting at midnight in the snowy woods, barefoot with only his dogs for company. His family was able to track him by following the bloody footprints he left behind in the snow.

Lewis showed a distinct preference for four-legged company over two. After the expedition passed the last white settlement of La Charette, Lewis established a routine of walking on shore with his Newfoundland dog Seaman, and occasionally a hunter or two, while Clark remained on board the keelboat. According to biographer Richard Dillon, Lewis was "a master of shanks' mare" and sometimes got so far ahead of the main party he was forced to camp by himself.

When it came to forming personal attachments among the enlisted men and the people they came into contact with, Lewis was always at a disadvantage: he preferred solitude to society. Lewis preferred the lonely scientific pursuits of gathering and describing specimens; he would rather be measuring the height of an anthill than engaging in conversation with other people. One of the saddest aspects of the end of Lewis's life is the fact that he had few friends other than William Clark; Jefferson had not heard from him in months. His final letter to James Madison in September 1809 shows that he had lost the ability to express himself through his writing, and he was surely at a loss when it came to conveying what Clark called "the waight of his mind" to anyone other than Clark himself. (Clark also received an alarming letter from Lewis that led him to believe early reports calling Lewis's death a suicide because they had "too much truth."[2])

Often called a form of highly functioning autism, Asperger's syndrome is a neurobiological disorder named for Hans Asperger, the Austrian physician who first documented it in the 1940s. Autism can be generally defined as a developmental disorder that appears before the age of three. Children with autism have difficulties with social interaction, communication, and exhibit a repetitive pattern of behaviors. Asperger's syndrome refers to a highly functioning form of autism. Autistic spectrum disorders have many forms ranging from severe to mild, and Asperger's syndrome is at the mild end of the spectrum. Dr. Asperger studied a group of boys who were of normal or above-average intelligence except for some autistic-like behaviors and delayed social and communicative skills. It is classified as a PDD, a pervasive developmental disorder characterized by severe and sustained impairment in social interaction and development of restricted and repetitive patterns of behavior, interests, and activities. People with this disorder tend to be hypersensitive to tastes, smells, sights, and sounds. They exhibit a distinct lack of empathy and a notable lack of common sense. They prefer routine and repetitive behaviors over change in every situation. On the other hand they are likely to be of above-average intelligence and highly proficient at whatever they chose to obsess over. Asperger's syndrome can be described as a communication disorder on two levels: reading and sending social or body language signals. People with it tend not to realize when people have stopped listening to their extremely detailed and minute descriptions. According to a recent article on the subject in the *Chronicle of Higher Education* (October 8, 2004), "People who have Asperger's tend to struggle with social interactions because of their extreme literal-mindedness. They typically are unable to infer meanings from tone or context. And when they lack explicit instructions on how to complete an assignment, some of them hit road blocks."

Because of their pronounced sensitivity and inability to decipher social cues, problems with anger and depression are commonly associated with Asperger's. Among other characteristics, according to Dr. Tony Attwood, noted authority on the disorder, "the cataloging of information about their specific interests is a way for them to make order out of chaos and cope with stress."[3]

As of 1994 Asperger's is listed in the main diagnostic reference of mental health professionals in the United States, the DSM-IV, and only recently have professionals, teachers, and parents started to develop effective treatment plans. As hard as it is for us "neuro-typicals" to understand, children with Asperger's have to be taught what a smile means.[4]

Anthropologist and Asperger's authority Dawn Prince-Hughes describes what it was like to grow up with Asperger's: "thinking in pictures" and "face blindness" were both typical features of the disorder. She writes of her struggle to appear normal although she lacked the ability to read or understand social cues and the facial expressions of others. Her intelligence was above normal, but she simply lacked the most fundamental part of being a human being: the ability to relate to other human beings.

Her life changed dramatically after a visit to Seattle's Woodland Park Zoo. She took a day off from dancing at a local strip club to seek some quiet and solitude at the zoo.

As she sat at the gorilla exhibit, she began to understand what it meant to be a sympathetic creature. In observing the nonthreatening interaction (no direct eye contact) between the gorillas over the next month, Prince-Hughes experienced an epiphany. She realized that all creatures shared a capacity for love and sympathy, and that hearts could speak to each other without words. The downward spiral of her life ended and she was able to use her talents for "keeping records, making keen observations, descriptively communicating and memorizing events perfectly" to earn a PhD in anthropology and, recently, to translate the Aspergerian world for the rest of us in her remarkable book *Songs of the Gorilla Nation*.

Lewis's biographers comment on the affection between the captain and his dog. Today we acknowledge the power of loving animals in treating afflictions from severe loneliness to autism. Therapy dogs have now been taught to detect oncoming seizures and even some forms of cancer in their owners. I believe Lewis and Seaman experienced such a bond. The journals mention the dog pleasing his master on more than one occasion with his excellent retrieval skills and by heroically rescuing the men from stampeding bison and the occasional marauding grizzly bear. There is plenty of evidence in the journals of the high regard Lewis held for his dog. When a beaver bit the dog's leg and severely injured him, Lewis worried, "I fear it will yet prove fatal to him."[5] And when he turned up missing one night Lewis wrote, "I was fearful that we had lost him altogether, however, much to my satisfaction he joined us at 8 o'clock this morning."[6]

It is rare to find Captain Meriwether Lewis admitting fear. When Seaman was stolen by the Natives, Lewis shows how far he would go for his beloved best friend. "Shoot them," he ordered the men if the Wah Cle-lah Indians hesitated to return his dog.

In a way, it seems that for Lewis, heading out alone, except for Seaman, for a twenty-mile stretch of the leg in the middle of a North Dakota winter was a form of therapy; he did it for himself as much as he did it to follow Jefferson's orders. He liked to maintain a wide "personal space," and perhaps he found the rhythm of walking comforting. On shore Lewis could collect samples, his way of imposing order, as if by killing a rattlesnake and then counting the "176 scuta on the belly and 17 scuta on the tale"[7] he could take away the threat of its lethal power.

At times Lewis writes in his journal as if he were on the outside looking in, a quality also associated with Asperger's. Many times it seems he is casting himself as the main character in a fairy tale. As evidence of his supersensitive hearing, Lewis takes time to describe the notes of a birdsong; he communicates with the "feathered tribes" on the Marias. At the Great Falls, where he met a menacing wolverine, three charging bison, and a grizzly bear, the "curious adventures wore the impression on my mind of inchantment" and "it now seemed to me that all of the beasts of the neighbourhood had made a league to destroy me, or that some fortune was disposed to amuse herself at my expence."[8]

That particular night Lewis preferred not to camp alone. He

calls the Shoshone "imps of Saturn" and grizzly bears "gentlemen." Commenting on a near-upset of the white pirogue he wrote, "I fear her evil genii will play so many pranks with her that she will go to the bottomm some of those days."[9]

When exploring the Marias, Lewis admitted he believed his chronometer stopped because "the fates were against me."[10]

On April 7, 1805, probably watching from the shore, Lewis wrote, "This little fleet altho' not quite so respectable as those of Columbus or Capt. Cook, were still viewed by us with as much pleasure as those deservedly famed adventurers ever beheld theirs; and I dare say with quite as much anxiety for their safety and preservation."[11]

Keep in mind that Asperger's is a spectrum disorder, part of a continuum of characteristics. Individuals may have varying degrees of any one or all of the characteristics. Some people with Asperger's view it as a gift, similar to genius; they see it more as a blessing and less as a curse. Authorities speculate that the very qualities that make people with Asperger's so strange are at the root of their peculiar talents. Thomas Jefferson appreciated Lewis's peculiar talents; he wrote, "It was if Lewis had been selected and implanted by nature"[12] to lead his Corps of Northwestern Discovery.

Lewis exhibited Asperger's tendencies early on. He had a pronounced habit of taking everything literally. This would ultimately serve him well when he received Jefferson's instructions as the captain of the expedition. When Lewis was a student he tested the theory of the earth's rotation by jumping up as high as he could; Dillon writes that he was disappointed to come down in the same place. In another notable episode the young Lewis stared down a charging bull and then shot him dead.

Asperger's causes clumsiness; according to cousin and schoolmate Peachy Gilmer, "his person was stiff and without grace, bow-legged, awkward, formal and almost without flexibility."[13]

Several times during the expedition Lewis nearly perished because he stood too close to the edge of a cliff.

In an environment they perceive as filled with too much noise and stimulation, people with Asperger's crave repetition and routine and are often shy and exhibit improper behavior. While in what one biographer called "the comic opera campaign" of the Whiskey Rebellion, Lewis thrived. Although he wrote his mother, "I am quite delighted with a soldier's life,"[14] he nevertheless got into some trouble later at Fort Grenville for provocative speech and gestures when he challenged a fellow officer to a duel. He was court-martialed for "abruptly and in an Ungentlemanlike manner, when intoxicated, entering his House . . . and disturbing the peace and harmony of a Company of Officers"[15] and then challenging one to a duel. Ultimately the court found him innocent, but anger would remain boiling just below the surface throughout Lewis's life. In a famous passage from a May 1804 letter to Clark, Lewis expresses his anger at Manuel Lisa in tangible terms:

Damn Manuel and triply Damn Mr. B. They give me more vexation and trouble than their lives are worth. I have dealt very plainly with these gentleman, in short I have come to an open rupture with them; I think them both great scoundrels, and they have given me abundant proofs of their unfriendly dispositions toward our government and its measures. These gentlemen (no I will scratch it out) these puppies, are not unacquainted with my opinions; and I am well informed that they have engaged some hireling writer to draught a petition and remonstrance to Govr. [of Louisiana Territory] Claiborne against me; strange indeed, that men to appearance in their senses, will show manifest such strong sumptoms of insanity, as to be wheting knives to cut their own throats.[16]

Attention to minute detail is a symptom of Asperger's, which is just what Lewis required as the chief supply officer of the Corps.

One extreme example of this tendency can be found earlier, in a 1798 letter Lewis wrote about his uniform to a fellow officer, complaining about the shoddy workmanship of a tailor who had made him a uniform coat:

Of all the damned pieces of work my coat exceeds. It would take up three sheets of paper, written in shorthand, to point out its deficiencies or, I may even say deformities. However, let it suffice that he has not lined the body at all; he had a galoon furnished for that purpose. The lace is deficient. I had it taken to pieces and altered and could I have done without it I should have returned it, beyond a doubt. For the blind button holes on the cuff he substituted lace and no part of those facings was worked blind. The four small buttons on the cape are deficient . . .[17]

Perhaps in part because of his attention to detail Lewis was appointed regimental paymaster, a job which enabled him to "ramble" as much as he said he yearned to. In a letter defending this trait to his mother Lewis writes, "I do not know how to account for this Quixotic disposition of mine in any other way than that of having inherited from the Meriwether family."[18]

Another reason for his appointment was his "natural head for figures" according to Dillon, and one more characteristic associated with Asperger's.

During his service as Thomas Jefferson's private secretary, certain elements of Lewis's character were encouraged by the president. He taught him how to read code using a specially designed alphabet. He recognized and encouraged his interest in the flora and fauna of Virginia and the eastern United States. When it became apparent that Lewis was Jefferson's logical choice to lead an expedition into the Louisiana Territory, and once Lewis received Jefferson's instructions, it is not an exaggeration to say that Lewis followed them to the letter. Indeed his journal entry from the day they departed from Fort Mandan shows he had the propensity for an "encompassing preoccupation," which is associated with Asperger's: "The picture which now presented itself to me was a most pleasing one, entertaining as I do the most confident hope of succeeding in a voyage which had formed a darling project of mine for the last ten years. I could but esteem this moment of my departure as among the most happy in my life."[19]

Throughout the expedition Lewis sees its successful outcome as a matter of his own personal survival. Without a triumphant return Lewis seems to feel that he would cease to exist. On the return journey, after he split his group into smaller and smaller units, Lewis sought the northernmost tributary of the Missouri, which Jefferson had instructed him to do, but he did so without the caution the president also required. To accomplish this misguided mission he headed up the Marias River with only three others into what he knew would be the most dangerous territory, and he encounters Blackfeet Indians, precisely what he says he is not looking for, then tells his men, "I should resist to the last extremity preferring death to that of being deprived of my papers instruments and gun desired that they would form the same resolution and be allert and on their guard."[20]

He seems to have forgotten Jefferson's stated instructions not to risk his life at any cost. Surely he did not have all the journals with him at this point. What happened to his common sense?

Certainly Lewis exhibited intelligence as well as a knack for imagining things constructed from the specific to the general and for "thinking in pictures." His designs for the keelboat, iron boat, gunpowder canisters, and Harper's Ferry rifle illustrate his talent at all things mechanical, also not an uncommon talent for people with Asperger's.

Dawn Prince-Hughes states that she used her intelligence to find ways to appear normal. One woman who was not diagnosed until in her late teens says she prided herself on appearing normal even though she knew she was different. Perhaps that happened with Lewis while he was in St Louis. According to Dillon, "he made friends with everyone" in St. Louis. How is that possible? Perhaps he realized that the success of his mission depended on gathering intelligence in St. Louis, intelligence that would be available only if he could be sociable. Despite the pronounced tendency of people with Asperger's to avoid eye contact, it seems that when he needed to, Lewis could interact with people in a more or less normal way. In other situations he was less forthcoming. One of the hallmarks of Asperger's is a profound discomfort with physical gestures associated with social interaction. When he first encountered the Shoshone in August 1805, for instance, he writes that the Natives embraced him so much that "we wer all carresed and besmeared with their grease and paint till I was heartily tired of the national hug."[21]

As examples of Lewis's lack of common sense, when collecting mineral samples he nearly poisoned himself "tasting" them. He made a highly questionable decision to leave a translator (Pierre Dorion) behind just as the opportunity for council presented itself, and he was inexplicably reluctant to give a bit of tobacco to the Teton Sioux in order to avoid a confrontation.

People with Asperger's often are unable to change their minds once they are set on a particular subject. Consider John Newman's expulsion for mutinous expression, for example. Lewis wrote, "The conduct of this man previous to this period had been generally correct, and the zeal he afterwards displayed for the benefit of the service was highly meritorious . . . he asked for forgivness for what had passed, and beged that I would permit him to continue with me through the voyage, but deeming it impolitic to relax from the sentence, altho' he stood acquitted in my mind, I determined to send him back, which was accordingly done."[22]

When it came to the winter stay of 1805–6 and the period of "uninterrupted friendly intercourse" with the Clatsop Indians, Lewis insisted the threat of their turning treacherous demanded constant vigilance: "Our preservation depends on never loosing sight of this trait in their character, and being always prepared to meet it in whatever shape it may present itself."[23]

People with Asperger's have difficulty seeing a middle ground in any argument and often feel more comfortable with black-and-white choices; gray areas create confusion and inertia. They can also lack social reciprocity. According to Manuel Lisa, his contemporary, Lewis was "fond of exaggerating everything relative to his expedition and . . . [was] a very headstrong & in many instances an imprudent man."[24] Charles McKenzie, an agent of the North West Company, commented that Lewis's prejudicial treatment of the British went further, stating he "could not make himself agreeable to us, he could speak fluently and learnedly on all subjects but his inveterate disposition against the British strained, at least in our eyes, all of his eloquence."[25]

U.S. attorney general Levi Lincoln wrote that he felt Lewis would be inclined to "push too far"[26] with regard to risking his own personal safety. In a letter to his brother Richard in 1809, secretary of the territory Frederick Bates wrote, "I never saw after his arrival in this country, anything in his conduct towards me but alienation and unmerited distrust."[27] Children with Asperger's often do not play well with others, and adults with the disorder have similar difficulties. We have no examples of Lewis participating in evening dances around the campfire and no record of him playing chase games with the troops or footraces with the Nez Perce, where Clark at least took part in the occasional shooting match.

Hampered by their social ineptitudes, people with Asperger's frequently appear immature. Living with the disorder is likened to an "eternal childhood," and as historian Clay Jenkinson writes in his study of the character of Meriwether Lewis, Lewis was "locked in an infantile stage." Evidence of this comes after a series of nearly fatal misadventures at the Great Falls of the Missouri, when Lewis admits that at that end of that most trying day he chose to confront three bison just to "at least give them some amusement."[28] On the Pacific Coast and in a rush to return home, he decided to steal a canoe from the coastal tribes and orders the burning of another canoe so that the Natives could not use it. After the encounter with the Blackfeet near the Marias River on the return journey, he burned the Blackfeet shields and "sundry items" and then decided to leave one of the last peace medals behind "so that they might be informed who we were."[29] He nearly tomahawked a Nez Perce man because the man had tossed a puppy into Lewis's lap or plate, which Lewis perceived as an insult; but perhaps the action was meant as a joke, and Lewis was incapable of "getting" it.

Another illustrative episode involves the reunion of Sacagawea and her childhood friend, which Lewis calls "really affecting," yet just two weeks earlier, he is unable to see or comprehend her emotions: "I cannot discover that she shows any emotion of sorrow in recollecting the event (of her capture) or of joy in being in her native country; if she has enough to eat and a few trinkets to wear I believe she would be perfectly content anywhere."[30]

When the baby Jean Baptiste Charbonneau is sick, Lewis refers to him as "it" in his journal entry. For a man who anthropomorphizes everything, including his gun and his boat, this is a bit more than surprising. But for a man afflicted with Asperger's it is symptomatic. It is Clark who makes the overtures of affection toward Jean Baptiste both during and after the expedition. One of the only times Lewis expresses sincere concern for his well-being is when his mother nearly died near the Great Falls and the idea of being responsible for a nursing infant suddenly seemed a distinct reality.

As his successor, Frederick Bates, said of Lewis, "his habits are altogether military & he never can I think succeed in any other profession."[31]

Behaviorists note that repetitive pursuits allow people with Asperger's to avoid the stress brought on by social contact. They long for the sameness of place and routine. But what if that sameness of place and routine were that of the road and of being king of the road? At the end of his life Lewis's finances were in a state of utter disarray. People with Asperger's tend to keep lots of daily tabs and records because it gives them the illusion of control. They believe their finances will eventually work themselves out. Lewis kept an account book in which he noted his debts, including several to Clark, who generously paid for medicine for Lewis's servant.

Historians often point to Lewis's ruminations in his journals on the occasion of his thirty-first birthday as revealing the true depths of his brooding personality. But what if you apply the Asperger's theory to his missive?

This day I completed my thirty first year, and conceived that I had in all human probability now existed about half the period which I am to remain in this Sublunary world. I reflected that I had as yet done but little, very little indeed, to further the happiness of the human race, or to advance the information of the succeeding generation. I viewed with regret the many hours I spent in indolence, and now soarly feel the want of that information which those hours would have given me had they been judiciously expended. But since they are past and cannot be recalled, I dash from me the gloomy thought and resolved in the future, to redouble my exertions and at least indeavour to promote those two primary objects of human existence, by giving them the aid of that portion of talents which nature and fortune have bestoed on me; or in future, to live for mankind, as I have heretofore lived for myself.[32]

Aspergerian tendencies are in evidence here. First, Lewis seems to be looking at his life from some distant perch, assessing himself as if he were judging one of his men or a younger brother. Another symptom is a strong belief in the validity and power of a pledge. Obviously Lewis is making a heartfelt pledge here, and he wants his readers to know it and presumably judge him favorably upon the completion of his tour.

Asperger's sufferers have a habit of writing things down and learning and recalling things through the act of writing. Lewis repeatedly exhibits a verbal proficiency often noted with Asperger's. (We will never know if Lewis's gaps in his journals resulted from loss or destruction or for some other reason.) His writings often display savant-like memorization faculties. Reading his journals and their descriptions of plants, animals, people, and places shows that Lewis had a way with words. However, he lacked confidence in his own way of phrasing things; many of his passages are unoriginal, as if he relied on others to frame his perceptions. Given his outstanding memory for the species back home, Lewis, according to Jefferson, "guarded by exact observation of the vegetables and animals of his own country against losing time in the description of objects already possessed."[33]

According to Temple Grandin, a professor at Colorado State University and livestock authority who has been diagnosed with Asperger's syndrome, the most comforting sensation for people with ASD is a constant pressure on the body. She designs cattle chutes and other livestock facilities and applied similar techniques when she designed a "squeeze machine" for herself. Perhaps the heavy bison robes Lewis slept under right up until his last night provided some level of comfort to him as well.

People with Asperger's have a strong sense of justice and equality. Lewis insisted that Clark receive the same rank as himself and the same compensation at the end of the journey.

Lewis's poor record in the romance department is often cited as evidence of his flawed character. According to one self-described "Aspie," living with Asperger's is like having an extreme male brain; they are even more systematic and more analytical than the average male. In a letter to Clark, Lewis referred to himself as "a musty, fusty, rusty, old bachelor,"[34] and he wrote to his friend Mahlon Dickerson declaring himself to be "a perfect widower with respect to love . . . I feel all that restlessness, that inquietude, that certain indescribable something common to old bachelors, which I cannot avoid thinking, my dear fellow, proceeds from that void in our hearts which might, or ought to be better filled. Whence it comes I know not, but certain it is that I never felt less like a hero than at the present moment. What may be my next adventure, God knows, but I am determined, to get a wife."[35]

Despite his stated intentions and his desirability as a marriageable prospect, Lewis failed miserably at love. It must have been a profound disappointment, as he surely had to be, on paper, one of the most desirable bachelors of his age. One woman, Letitia Brackenridge, was so alarmed by his intentions in Fincastle, Virginia, that she made a hasty retreat to Richmond. Editor Donald Jackson noted that Lewis's search for a wife was "dogged and inexplicably futile." It seems plausible that he was unlucky at love because Asperger's led him to "look through" people, avoid social contact, not know what to do or how to mingle with other people. His awkwardness and lack of emotional intelligence was so pronounced it was off-putting, especially to the opposite sex. Yet people with Asperger's have difficulties with the full range of human relationships, not just those with the opposite sex. In Lewis's case it may account for why he never kept a domestic slave as close to him as Clark kept York. Even the intimacy of a master-slave relationship was difficult for him.

At the end of his life, Lewis lost his bearings. He lost touch with Jefferson, who wrote letters rebuking him for not getting to work on the journals. He no longer followed a familiar routine and medicated himself with alcohol and other drugs. He was alone except for his brother and perhaps his dog. Here was a man who once wrote that he held it a crime to anticipate evil now having to face the possibility of dishonor and public humiliation. His attempts at finding a wife had failed miserably. Asperger's often causes depression and anger because of the frustration of trying to fit in. Lewis thrived in the military and in leading the expedition because he knew just where he fit in and exactly where he stood. He could ramble on the shore with his favorite companion and count the feathers on a bird, the scales on a fish, or the scuta on a rattlesnake tail. He could write page after page of detailed scientific descriptions that he believed would surely be of great import someday. While following Jefferson's instructions, his life had order, balance, repetition, and routine. He could be aloof and in command at the same time. His problems came when routine disintegrated and he was forced to have more and more direct contact with other people who were unfamiliar with his idiosyncrasies. The man who a few years earlier carried the most valuable letter of credit in the Western world was suddenly being forced to justify his own expenses and those associated with the return of the Mandan chief Sheheke-shote to the Upper Missouri. His honor was in question. Lewis was on his way to plead his case when he made his fateful stop on the Natchez Trace.

As a woman with Asperger's describes it, her fantasy was to flee to Scandinavia:

Because of its foreignness it was totally opposite to any one and anything known to me. That was my escape, a dream world where nothing would remind me of daily life and all it had to throw at me. The people from this wonderful place look totally unlike any people in the "real world." Looking at these faces, I could not be reminded of anyone who might have humiliated, frightened, or rebuked me. The bottom line is I was turning my back on real life and its ability to hurt, and escaping.[36]

In the end I think Lewis was heartily tired of more than national hugs. I think he was simply worn out by the day-to-day demands of living in society while possibly suffering from Asperger's, and so, according to Thomas Jefferson, "did the deed which plunged his friends into affliction and deprived his country of one of her most valued citizens."[37] Had he lived in our time perhaps he would have received the therapy and treatment he needed to integrate himself into society. It is a moot point now. We will never know whether Meriwether Lewis suffered from Asperger's syndrome or what caused him to take his own life. We do know that he was missed, and that in spite of his complex personality, he was loved, and by more than man's best friend.

9. Why Sacagawea Deserves the Day Off

I take issue with those who say Sacagawea has emerged the winner in the Bicentennial Idol sweepstakes. I see the winner of that contest to be William Clark, who after two hundred years of being in Lewis's shadow finally achieved the recognition he deserved in the form of two new scholarly biographies and a panel at the National Signature Event at Pompey's Pillar in 2006.

What would she think of us two hundred years later, meeting in Bismarck, North Dakota, or Pocatello, Idaho, to understand what her life meant to the history of the United States? How come she gets left holding the bag for a laundry list of interest groups even to this day? Empire builders; white apologists; feminists; Christians; governments tribal, federal, state, and local; and even the U.S. Mint seem to have ulterior motives when it comes to the way they seek to use her memory.

Why do we want her as our endorser, as our poster girl for causes and interests from A to Z? I am surprised People for the Ethical Treatment of Animals haven't yet used her image in a campaign. Tradition has it that even though famished she passed on eating dog.

We have statues of her, more statues than any other woman, not to mention rivers, streams, peaks, lakes, hot springs, and mountains named in her honor. We have countless schools, a constellation, a navy ship, a plane, plazas, a scenic byway, hotels, books, DVDs, a stamp, a coin, a candy bar, and a perfume. She has her own brand of decaf coffee with a label of her smiling and winking and holding a cup of hot coffee over the line "worth the journey." I understand she was recently given her own hazel nut, and that somewhere in Washington State is the Sacagawea Industrial Park. (I personally am waiting for her to get her own shoe, kind of like the Mary Jane only this one would be the Janey.) But do any of these celebrate the real woman, or are they all monuments to someone who never existed, to someone who might rightly be labeled pure fiction?

After years of our molding and imagining her character, I say it is time we gave Sacagawea her own holiday. By this I do not mean a day off from work or school for us, but a day off for her. On National Sacagawea Day we would relieve her of the burdens we have foisted onto her for no other reason than that her story is inspiring. Let's relieve her of the burden of being a national icon. Let's give her credit for being who she was, not for whom we want her to be. No pointy-fingered statues, no U.S. currency, no postage stamp, no hazel nut, and certainly no industrial park.

We need to set her free from the burden of our collective fantasies. Who was she really? What do we know about her? Why do we care about her? As for what we know there are a handful of descriptions, mainly from Clark, who said she was lighter in skin color than Charbonneau's other wife, that she was particularly useful, and that her patience was truly admirable. Lewis once said her fortitude and resolution in an emergency were equal to that of the rest of the Corps and named a river in her honor. We know that her first experience with childbirth was long and tedious (Lewis's word) and that she preferred wintering where the potas roots grew. We know she insisted on getting permission to go with the party that was going to see the ocean and the whale beached there. In present-day Montana, near Bozeman, Clark called her "the Indian woman who has been of great service to me as a pilot through this country." And Henry Brackenridge, who traveled with the Charbonneaus when they returned to the Knife River Villages from St. Louis in 1811, said she was "a good creature of a mild and gentle disposition." At the end of the expedition Clark said, in a letter to Charbonneau, "Your woman who accompanied you that long, dangerous and fatiguing rout deserved a greater reward."

Many see her role as insignificant, certainly not historically relevant, and nowhere near the girl-guide portrayed in popular literature. I see her as a young woman who knew where she belonged; even after some five years' absence followed by a dramatic reunion, she knew that her home was with her husband, the father of her child, and that is where she stayed for the rest of her life. When it came to allegiances, I think, she would say hers was more to Charbonneau than to a specific tribe.

Sacagawea likely never had a day off in her real life. She would have been part of the communal labor force of the Hidatsa women responsible for planting, harvesting, gathering, butchering, tanning, and sewing, as well as maintaining the earth lodge. I imagine she was adroit at all of these tasks and friendly enough with the rest of the women that she would even stand up for one, once, when she needed defending. If we were to spend a day with Sacagawea in her village at the Knife River I think we would all be surprised at how clean, orderly, and organized their lives were. The women maintained the crops and passed down the right to plant them in certain areas through their daughters. When it came to actual physical labor the women contributed more than their share, but they owned the fruits of their labor as well. As Virginia Roberts Peters points out in her book *Women of the Earth Lodges*, these women worked from sunup to sundown because they had few labor-saving devices. They cooked the food, made and fixed the clothing, and maintained the shelter for the family, and most of them took pride in their work and enjoyed doing their best at a given task. In some ways you could call the area around the Mandan villages, during Sacagawea's lifetime, the Sam's Club of the Great Plains. Because they were able to produce a surplus of corn, the Mandan-Hidatsa had a prominent place in the local economy, and all of this relied on the labor of women. To be sure the men had their roles, including hunting, horse-tending, politicking, and raiding, but it was the women of the Earth Lodges who provided the sweat equity. There were rewards in Sacagawea's world, belts and other forms of personal adornment that would be worn with pride because they signified a job well done.

Perhaps to Sacagawea's mind the notion of having the day off would mean you were either sick or menstruating. The rest of the time she would have been engaged in the day-to-day chores, rituals, and games that made up Mandan and Hidatsa life. Her situation might have been unique because she was married to a trader and interpreter, but as Harold Howard points out in his biography *Sacagawea*, that was the pinnacle of many young Native American girls' ambitions at that time. Perhaps Charbonneau, rather than degrading her through the "purchase" or winning of her might have elevated her status a bit. Certainly becoming a mother gave her a place in the world and a reason to never give up.

So the concept of a day off as applied to Sacagawea needs a bit broader context. I propose giving her a day off from groups and organizations trying to plant their flagpoles on her heart and etch their allegiances and trademarks onto her forehead. A "Free Sacagawea" march could be held. We could have bumper stickers, and Jack Gladstone could write us an anthem. It is like when we hear old Beatles tunes used in commercials or see dead celebrities hawking products in special-effects-generated commercials. There is something that makes us want to say YUCK.

We need add nothing to nor take anything away from the record on Sacagawea. Her accomplishments and talents speak for themselves.

I personally would like her to pardon us for taking her history as a living, breathing person away and substituting it with 80 percent myth, legend, and fantasy. Pardon us for casting you as a torchbearer or guilt-holder for all kinds of causes you had no knowledge of or opinion on and which in fact you might have objected to if given the chance.

Forgive us for endlessly debating the spelling and meaning of your name. I imagine if you knew the extent to which that discussion continues you would want to take a long shower. Surely there is more to examine in your life than the origin, meaning, and spelling of your name. Your parents and family knew it and you knew it. Enough said.

I do not assume she would object to all of these memorials and accolades. I simply think she would wonder at the sheer variety and number of them, at the good old American overkill. What would she make of a beanie baby named after her? Or an American Girl doll or a candy bar? Or a decaf coffee? Likely she preferred tea.

On National Sacagawea Day no one could make jokes or ridicule the coin commissioned in her honor. Why should her memory be contaminated by a coin everyone loves to hate? And believe me they do love to hate it. Many businesses resorted to giving them away when the general public seemed unimpressed and refused to use them.

Again I ask that we reconsider the historical Sacagawea and give her credit for who she was. For example, although in popular culture she is celebrated as a guide, we do not celebrate her greater genius, which would seem to be her memory for landscapes, her ability to translate between highly different languages and worldviews, and her understanding of harvesting foods and moccasin reading. In modern times she might have been an engineer or a crime scene investigator or a foreign correspondent with those skills. In her world landmarks told stories and because of that they stayed fixed in her mind. Think of Beaverhead Rock. She remembered those places because as a young child she would travel there with her people looking for bison and roots. These travels were based on the seasons and the stories associated with the places they went. The landmarks told stories, and Sacagawea must have been a very good listener.

And observer. When it comes to being the champion observer of the expedition, most folks feel no one holds a candle to Meriwether Lewis. But several times during the expedition Sacagawea proves to be in his league. She noted where the bark of a ponderosa pine tree had been harvested by Natives, and she likely knew where to find the wild artichokes stashed by the prairie mice. She gave Lewis the bitterroot and showed him how to eat it; she gave Clark the white apple and the fennel root, which he also credited her with finding.

I think she often gets shortchanged in acknowledgment concerning her talents as a mother. The fact that nowhere in the journals is there a complaint about an inconsolable infant testifies to her talent and instinct as a mother. Who was there for her to ask advice? She depended on what she had observed in both the Lemhi Shoshone and the Hidatsa cultures to know how to take care of and raise her son. The proof of her goodness as a mother can be seen in the life of her son, who went on to be a highly qualified guide and interpreter in his adult life.

Some people marvel at her endurance. They can't believe that a woman could keep up with a bunch of hardy young soldiers. Well, what if they had a hard time keeping up with her? I think Clark gives her a pat on the back for her endurance when he writes in his letter to Charbonneau that she accompanied him on the long, dangerous, and fatiguing route.

But she needs no defenders.

Maybe most of the claims we stake on Sacagawea's memory are because we want her to be our friend. We want her approval, her glad tidings, her ermine tails, her stale bread, her lump of sugar, her blue-beaded belt, all of the gifts she gave. We want to hold them close. Imagine if that blue-beaded belt were somehow found and put on the market today. It might fetch more than the iron boat on eBay!

We want her friendship for the very reason John Luttig noted when she died at Fort Manuel in 1812. "She was a good and the best woman of the fort." Her integrity was intrinsic; she needs no mythology or statue. From the very beginning of her appearance in the journals she stood for something without perhaps even knowing it. Yet she was the real thing.

A woman. A mother. A wife and a sister, a friend, a woman who knew where she belonged. A woman who was strong, worked hard, and loved her children. None of these things necessarily makes her a hero, but in a sense it makes her the best kind of hero: one we can recognize and celebrate in ourselves. So let's pull up our claim stakes, pull out our flagpoles, and finally after all these years let her have a day off, let her rest in peace, let her lay down all of the burdens collected from sea to shining sea.

That said, there are a few intriguing mysteries about Sacagawea I would like to explore.

How did they get her to give up her belt—one of her few and certainly one of her most valuable possessions? Whitehouse tells us that her belt was used to trade for a sea otter robe admired by the captains. Clark tells us she was given a blue cloth coat in return for her belt. Seems someone got rooked here. Perhaps it was Charbonneau who persuaded her by convincing her it would be for the good of the whole party. "Come on, honey, it will make the captain happy and I promise to get you a better one as soon as we get back to Knife River." I have seen a highly romanticized version of that transaction showing Sacagawea lovingly placing her blue-beaded belt into Clark's hands as she gazed longingly into his eyes. Reality check! I imagine she was less than happy that particular day, and I doubt she appreciated giving up two of her leather suits (dresses) for a horse later on. I find it interesting that the particular "handsomely dressed sea otter robe" ended up in Lewis's personal affects when he died in Tennessee. We don't know what happened to Lewis's prized souvenir but we do know that her belt would probably be worth a fortune today.

What was her relationship to Lewis? His dismissal of her by saying that if she had a few trinkets and some food to eat she could be happy anywhere was no doubt meant as an insult. In some ways it also seems to qualify her as a good soldier. I think their relationship was strained but that he did respect her, especially after she saved the "light articles" when the white pirogue nearly capsized. I think he worried about her when she got sick but mainly because he knew if she died his chances of securing horses from the Shoshone would be low. She could not know that in his journal Lewis would refer to her son as "it." I think if she fully understood his implication she would be highly insulted. Months before at Fort Clatsop Sacagawea gave twenty-four white weasel tails to Captain Clark, which I read as her voting as to who was the true leader of the expedition at that point. I am not sure he would have credited her with the "instinctual sagacity" he gave to the Nez Perce guides, but clearly both captains recognized that she was a walking peace token and as such was instrumental in the friendly receptions they received. In the end, I doubt that she mattered to Lewis in any personal way, but I'm sure he would be willing to admit she earned her place in history, if not alongside him at least on the same page. And he might even admit that she taught him a thing or two.

What was her marriage like? When Sacagawea was ill at the Great Falls, there is a line in the journals that says, "Charbonneau petitions to return," meaning that they weren't going to cure her so he wanted to take her back and have the Hidatsa try to save her. This one line says volumes about the way Charbonneau cared for Sacagawea. She was more than a slave or a possession to him, and he must have been, in some sense, desperate to save her. A few days later, when she has recovered enough to eat and eats too much, Captain Clark blames Charbonneau. I can see him saying, "Mon dieu, Captain! She won't listen to me either!" As for her feelings for him, she stayed by his side, even after returning to her own people, until death parted them.

Why didn't Lewis have her with him when he first approached the Shoshone in August 1805? Perhaps because Clark was ailing, but there is no doubt that Lewis wanted to be first; he wanted to be the leader that day. And if Sacagawea had come along, Clark would have been there, too. Lewis wanted to be out in front, as he often did in times of anticipated "discovery." He did use information gleaned from Sacagawea to ease the fears of the Shoshone he encountered. He repeated the words "tab a boin," which he understood to mean white man, and in a gesture of peace he learned from Sacagawea, he "painted the tawny cheeks of the women with vermillion." So even though she was not there during that pivotal moment she did influence the outcome.

What was her favorite part of the trail? After years of considering this and discussing it with many of her fans, I think it would have had to be on the Yellowstone River. Despite the mosquitoes and worrying that they were going to eat her son alive, I think she liked being useful in finding the way to the river over Bozeman Pass. I feel certain Clark would have told her he named Pompey's

Pillar for her son, and the fact that he carved his name on it must have meant something to her. Personally I love that site because it forever links Clark with the Charbonneau family and it says most eloquently that they were his friends.

Could she have died of a broken heart? Regarding the death of Sacagawea in 1812 I have always been curious about it but not for the obvious reason. My curiosity stems from the proximity of her death to the time of leaving her son in St. Louis with William Clark. As a mother myself, I can think of nothing more gut-wrenching and stress-inducing than leaving your only child behind.

What if we had an account of their parting? We know that the two cultures she lived in, Lemhi Shoshone and Hidatsa, valued family ties and mothers' roles as particularly important. Given the circumstances of their time together it is not unreasonable to assume she and her son shared an extremely close bond. How is it that in less than a year after leaving him in St. Louis she was dead? Brackenridge says she had become sickly and longed to revisit her native country. But what if she died of a broken heart? Having just delivered her second child, her first, her dancing boy, the one she loved more than any other, was probably the last thing on her mind as she left this world. It makes sense to me, but that is only because I am sentimental about such things, and when you study and write history it is best to leave sentiment at the door. But who wouldn't prefer dying of a broken heart to "putrid fever"?

Finally, I think we cannot help but romanticize Sacagawea. She is simply too unique. We will always want her to be our friend, to hold our flag, to be our symbol. We want to be like her, to have patience and fortitude and a mild manner.

Even though it is tempting to think of her getting a reprieve, a National Sacagawea Day Off, there are too many of us, myself included, who can never surrender the version of her we cooked up in our minds. She will continue to mean this to you and that to me, continue to be what someone once called a human Rorschach test. But maybe with continued rigorous scholarship we can come a little closer to the true woman and what she really means to America.

Clark always wanted to give her a greater reward, and in one way she has it. Young people continue to be inspired by her example. Each new generation of children discovers her and wants to know more about her. They want to be her friend.

I recently read a story about children portraying their favorite historical characters. Vanessa Rodriquez, nine, spoke of her kinship with her favorite historical figure. "I sort of look like her," she said of Sacagawea, "she can speak many languages and she has a strong heart." The article went on to say that portraying Sacagawea made Vanessa think about being more patient when she translated English for her Spanish-speaking cousins. Obviously Vanessa has her own version of Sacagawea, and it helps her and gives her strength, just as my version continues to do for me.

A few summers ago I was at Beaverhead Rock thinking about her and wondering what she would think of the bicentennial and all of the attention her memory continues to receive. I think she would say, "Go ahead and have your party, play the fiddle, shoot off the fireworks, and raise the glass, but don't forget that I was a real person made of flesh and bone, just like you. I need no extra credit for things I never did. And please NO MORE POINTY-FINGERED STATUES!"

10. Beyond Measuring Shadows
What Would Thomas Jefferson Do?

If you examine it in its simplest of terms, the Lewis and Clark Expedition represents a giant census taking, an accounting, a summing up of what was out there so as to claim and better tend it, to make it useful and ultimately commercially profitable. The legacy of that survey and all of its implications for the future is for us and for subsequent generations to figure out. What is the proper response to wild places disappearing? How can we honestly explain that to our children?

I want to begin by looking at how Jefferson regarded nature. In a letter to his friend, the artist, naturalist, and collector Charles Willson Peale, Jefferson states, "No occupation is so delightful to me as the culture of the earth, and no culture comparable to that of the garden. Such a variety of subjects, some always coming to perfection, the failure of one thing repaired by the success of another, and instead of one harvest a continued one through the year. Under a total want of demand except for our family table, I am still devoted to the garden. But though an old man, I am but a young gardener."

In 1813, two years later, he picked up the theme again in a letter to Peale: "The spontaneous energies of the earth are a gift of nature, but they require the labor of man to direct their operation. And the question is so to husband his labor as to turn the greatest quantity of earth to his benefit. Plowing deep, your recipe for killing weeds is also the recipe for almost every good thing in farming. The plow is to the farmer what the wand is to the sorcerer. Its effect is really like sorcery."

So it is not surprising that Jefferson's proudest invention was an improved plow board, in 1788, for which he won a gold medal from the French Society of Agriculture. In addition to offering the least resistance as it was pulled through the soil, Jefferson's invention had a further advantage, as he wrote to Sir John Sinclair in 1798, "It may be made by the coarsest workman, by a process so exact, that its form shall never be varied by a single hair's breadth."

Coming to terms with Jefferson's view of nature is no easy task. Like everything associated with him, the seemingly simple ends up being intensely complicated. Just when you think you have pinned him down, he offers a contradiction. For instance, consider his reverence for a ninety-foot span of stone bridging Cedar Creek in Rockbridge County, Virginia, called the Natural Bridge. The 215-foot-tall formation cost Jefferson twenty shillings when he purchased it in 1774 to ensure that it remained available to the public. In a revealing passage in *Notes on the State of Virginia* Jefferson describes his beloved Natural Bridge as the most sublime of Nature's works, but he writes:

Though the sides of this bridge are provided in some parts with a parapet of fixed rocks yet few men have the resolution to walk to them and look over the abyss. You involuntarily fall on your hands and feet to creep to the parapet and peep over it. Looking down from this height for about a minute gave me a violent head ach. If the view from the top be painful and intolerable that from below is delightful in an equal extreme. It is impossible for the emotions arising from the sublime, to be felt beyond what they are here; so beautiful an arch, so elevated, so light springing as it were up to heaven, the rapture of the spectator is really indescribable.

After he purchased it from King George III, he maintained and publicized it and intended it to remain a permanent, publicly accessible feature. Today it is one of our most treasured National Historic Landmarks. Historian Donald Jackson writes that for Jefferson the Natural Bridge was his "Royal Gorge, his Great Falls, his own sampling of the wonderlands of America." Although Jefferson visited it throughout his life, Charles Miller points out in his book *Jefferson and Nature* that "Jefferson's home was next to Monticello not the Natural Bridge ... his faith lay in technology, individual freedom, and the stages of development expected even of the Indians."

Jefferson, under the influence of his surveyor father, Peter, and his father's Loyal Land Company, believed that to have an understanding of an uncharted wilderness you first needed an inventory. His letter of instructions to Meriwether Lewis carefully laid out a monumental task: discover everything about the Upper Missouri and Columbia River drainages. "Along with finding the most direct and practicable water communication across the continent for purposes of commerce," he wrote, Lewis was to observe "the soil and face of the country, its growth and vegetable productions, the animals of the country generally & especially those not known in the U.S."

The president particularly wanted an account of any animals that may be "deemed rare or extinct." Jefferson sought to win a theoretical argument with the Count de Buffon of France, who insisted that because parts of America experienced a warm and moist climate, the animals of the New World had degenerated and would be inferior in size and strength to those of the Old. Jefferson hoped his explorers would bring him back the bones he needed to win the debate. Another reason for his interest in rare animals concerned the theory of extinction. As historian Daniel Boorstin points out in *The Lost World of Thomas Jefferson*, for Jefferson, no species of animal ever had or ever could become extinct. He wanted his expedition to prove that the mammoth and megalonyx, or great claw, still existed somewhere in the vastness of the West. To him, finding bones was not proof that a species had once existed; it was proof that it still existed.

When Jefferson presented his *Memoir on the Discovery of Certain Bones of a Quadruped of the Clawed Kind in the Western Parts of Virginia* to the Philosophical Society in 1797 he stated, "In fine the bones exist; therefore the animal has existed. The movements of nature are in a never ending circle. The animal species which has once been put into a train of motion is still probably moving in that train. For if one link in nature's chain might be lost, another and another might be lost, till the whole system of things would evanish piece meal."

Jefferson's obsession with the mammoth and the great claw whetted his appetite for the collection of animal bones. When he gave Lewis instructions for his expedition, perhaps Jefferson eagerly imagined that his explorers would come around the bend in a river and encounter a mammoth out for an evening stroll. If it seems fanciful to us, his curiosity is at the heart of the conception of the expedition and accounts for some of the continued fascination with it to this day. It is not so much that they discovered new species, which they certainly did; it was that Jefferson anticipated mountains of salt, active volcanoes, the lost tribes of Israel, and gargantuan mammoths waiting to be exposed to civilization.

Jefferson firmly believed that because of what he called "the economy of Nature" there could be no extinction. In his universe evolution did not occur, because it would upset the rational order of things. Yet within one generation, two of the bird species that the captains noted on their journey in great number had become extinct. The passenger pigeon and the Carolina parakeet went the way of the dinosaurs.

I earlier mentioned Jefferson's only book-length work, his *Notes on the State of Virginia*. Written in 1781, it was developed in answer to a questionnaire given by a French diplomat to each delegate at the Continental Congress. Along with a map, it contains his observations on every aspect of the Virginia environment. A status report sprinkled with the moral and ethical principles of the author, its sum is much more important than its parts. Described by biographer Charles Miller as "veering wildly from tables of Indian populations, names of plants, and weather data to hymns to the Natural Bridge and the independent farmer," it has also been called a "testament of freedom which constitutes a significant page in the history of man's efforts to free himself, through knowledge from the shackles of the past." Typically, Jefferson intended to update and revise it over time, but other projects distracted him. In 1814 he wrote to a publisher, "I consider . . . the idea of preparing a new copy [of *Notes*] as no more to be entertained. The work itself indeed is nothing more than the *measure of a shadow*, never stationary, but lengthening as the sun advances, and to be taken anew from hour to hour. It must remain, therefore for some other hand to sketch its appearance at another epoch, to furnish another element for calculating the course and motion of this member of our federal system."

Along with inventories and observations on his environment, Jefferson's inventions and interest in the gadgets of his day reveal a man who believed that all problems could be solved. Yet he could deny that there was such a thing as extinction because to accept it would mean, perhaps, accepting his and our own tenuous place in the universe, in nature. By sending his agents into the uncharted wilderness Jefferson was not only claiming the land for the United States, he was claiming for the American Enlightenment victory over nature itself. His men could go the distance, face the obstacles, and send back neatly cataloged samples for his collection at Monticello. One of his later explorers, Zebulon Pike, sent him a pair of live grizzly bear cubs for his collection in 1807; he gave them to Charles Willson Peale for his Great School of Nature museum in Philadelphia. After one of them trapped Peale's family in their living quarters, he shot them. You can take the grizzly bear out of the wild but not the wild out of the grizzly bear.

For Jefferson, nature was something man improved through farming, and while he admired the sublime in nature, I sense he admired most its ability to inspire great thoughts in himself. Witness his description of the Natural Bridge, which astute observers note that Lewis echoed when he described the Great Falls. Jefferson understood that nature's economy and abundance allowed him, through farming, to care for himself and his family as much as any other Virginia slave-owning planter was able to do.

To Jefferson, nature made sense; he had issues with those areas of natural science that did not fit neatly into his worldview. He called geology "the study of scratches on the earth" and regarded it as "too idle to be worth a single hour of any man's life." He would have seen no need for paleontology because recovered bones indicated a live species, not an extinct one. "What difference does it make if the world is 600 or 6000 years old?" he once asked. He had faith that in the future we would find the answers. Today, faced as we are with holes in the ozone and cancer-causing substances in the environment, the fear is that we will run out of time before we find those answers.

And what would Jefferson have made out of our national parks? What would he have thought of the Endangered Species Act or the Wilderness Act? Would he have favored restoring wild salmon runs? We know that Lewis and Clark did not practice modern conservation methods when they collected specimens to send back to the president. But to their credit, I think, they did remind the men that wanton slaughter would not be tolerated despite the large herds of ungulates as far as the eye could see. Jefferson's preservation, and indeed worship, of the Natural Bridge indicates that he would have understood the need for conservation and preservation. I think he would have understood the Upper Missouri River Breaks National Monument and supported its designation, though some may disagree with me. Such is the character of Thomas Jefferson. Here was a man who did not want any one branch of government to make decisions on its own, yet he alone authorized the Louisiana Purchase.

As my bookshelves groan under the weight of new titles on Lewis and Clark, I think of Jefferson and his four libraries and how he loved learning. His *Notes on the State of Virginia*, the journals he commissioned, and the efforts of modern-day conservation groups have much in common. They represent an abiding faith in the future and in a scholarly tradition we should all take seriously. They are more than the "measure of a shadow." They are a legacy in every sense of the word. At least every two hundred years we need to make a head count. We need to file a status report in the name of Thomas Jefferson. We need to make a list! We need to find out where the chain is weak so that we can strengthen it.

I need no convincing when it comes to preserving and protecting what is left along the trail. I am instinctively against threats to the salmon migration along the Snake River, tire-burning dumps near Three Forks, and coal plants on the Portage site. I supported the designation of the Upper Missouri River Breaks National Monument. I rejoiced when the land around Traveler's Rest acquired permanent protection. I was thrilled when more than fifty thousand people said they did not want gas wells and industrial development on the Rocky Mountain Front and the government responded. That is the legacy I want to leave my children. Several summers ago I enjoyed a visit to a churchyard in Philadelphia where descendants of the Osage orange seeds Lewis collected shade the graves of some of Jefferson's friends, including Peale. While in Philadelphia we also visited the Liberty Bell, where I was surprised to find myself genuinely moved. It struck me that if "We the People" can recognize and appreciate the symbols associated with our democratic roots we should also find some way of doing the same for places in America that are just as prone to cracking as our beloved old bell. As it so eloquently testifies, fixing cracks is a whole lot harder than preventing them in the first place.

The trail will always need to be protected. We need to work with groups like the Montana Wilderness Association, the Nature Conservancy, American Rivers, the Sierra Club, Friends of the Missouri Breaks, the Clark Fork Coalition—the list goes on. We desperately need their help, along with the help of local Lewis and Clark Trail Heritage Foundation chapters, tribal representatives, NPS-qualified guides, and even talented musicians like Jack Gladstone and Rob Quist. We need them to show us how to walk softly as we collect memories along the trail. We must help visitors move from what University of Montana professor Albert Borgman called the "disengaged state" to an engaged state, to see themselves as a part of a chain. We need to teach visitors about the fragility of nature, about the impact humans have had on nature, about nature's resilience, and how to encourage it to thrive. We need to help groups like the Wappato Society in Washington State, which is dedicated to the preservation of a rare root that the Indians foraged and that is mentioned in the journals, and the folks who are protecting and reseeding the native grasses on the Spirit Mound, and all who are working to save endangered plants, animals, and fishes from extinction.

As a person who lives in a state known as "The Last Best Place," it probably comes as no surprise that for most of my adult life I have been involved in conservation and environmental battles. I learned about the good fight when we successfully "Banned the Bomb," the seismic exploration in the Bob Marshall Wilderness Area. You can say that I am a certified tree hugger and I won't mind a bit. Blame it on Lewis and Clark, or on Jefferson, who was known to have "pet trees" at Monticello. I am not saying Lewis and Clark were America's first enviros. I am saying that because they followed Jefferson's orders and the example he supplied in his *Notes*, their faithful recordings of what the Great Northern Plains looked like in the early 1800s paint a convincing portrait of a thriving economy of nature involving man, bison, and native grasses, part of what some tribes called the Great Circle. And believe it or not there are areas in Montana where those native grasses still grow and have never been tilled. We have been in a "wilderness drought" in my state for twenty years; I am excited that recent events promise a change in the wind. While it is not always easy to persuade the "fiercely independent" citizens of the West that wanton resource extraction is not part of the right to pursue happiness, we need to protect special places and resources before they disappear like the Carolina parakeet. As one conservation group points out, "We need wilderness and now Wilderness needs us to protect and preserve the values of Wilderness that are essential to our own well-being and survival. Saving Wilderness, we save ourselves."

How do we convey the feeling of value and worthiness to something as large and as all-encompassing as the Lewis and Clark Trail? The same way they do it in Philadelphia with the Liberty Bell. We do not all need to be experts on the minute details, but we do need to understand the big picture. Historical and cultural places like the Rocky Mountain Front need protection, period.

Coming to terms with the legacy of Lewis and Clark's list includes acknowledging their treatment of Native peoples. Here again we must be thankful for the record they left, but we must be willing to listen to the accounts from the other side. As historian Harry Fritz has said, after two hundred years of white males hogging the mike it is time for the Native Americans to tell their side. If that means listening to the many and often conflicting accounts, so be it. That is part of the legacy. It is time to move beyond the captains' dismissal of Native American creation stories as mere "superstition." We need to figure out what lessons the stories are really trying to teach. This part of the story is a true legacy. Jefferson's fascination with Indian languages was an integral part of his fascination with the West. He wanted the captains to collect as many examples of the languages as they could. With all the attention generated by the commemoration of the trail bicentennial, it may be that some of those very languages he sought to collect are going to be saved.

Getting to the core of the Corps is a never-ending task. Each generation sculpts the figures of Lewis and Clark into the statue it needs to revere at that particular time. Some overlying truths do emerge, and they probably echo Jefferson's feeling that extinction did not exist; but we know that black holes are out there, and that our understandings do evolve. That is the legacy of Lewis and Clark's list and the work done to designate and preserve wilderness areas: they affirm that we are evolving. Slowly but surely we are learning to seek a balance with nature. Jefferson wanted us to study the economy of nature and from that study move closer to the perfection of the Creator. I think he would be grateful, as I am, to all of the individuals, agencies, and groups who work for conservation and who help us to "proceed on" with that task.

11. New Beginnings
Why We Still Need Lewis and Clark

Among the afflicted Lewis and Clark devotees at most gatherings I am arguably the most so. I attended six or seven signature events of the trail bicentennial commemoration and likely traveled, in temperatures ranging from near 0 to 110, at least the eight thousand miles the Corps of Discovery covered. I think I have just about every commemorative pin and every other kind of memorabilia from most of the events of the last three years. My favorite is the peace medal I received at the first signature event at Monticello. A reenactor from Kentucky made the authentic trade bead necklace and fastened it on my neck.

It should come as no surprise, therefore, that I am unwilling to look at the culmination of the commemoration through any other lens than as a beginning, or at least a jump start, on many levels.

It was the beginning of a growing realization among the general public that distinct American Indian tribes existed then and remain with us today: "We are still here," tribes like to say, and in many states other than Montana, where I live, that represents a novel idea. It was the beginning of another revelation: that casinos may not be as much of a cure-all as the general public might presume them to be. American Indian reservations continue to face the laundry list of problems. They are displaced persons in their own country, an irony Americans are just beginning to come to terms with. It was the beginning of what University of Montana history professor Harry Fritz said is "the Indians' turn to take over the mike" after two hundred years of white voices hogging it for themselves.

It was the beginning of a new recognition among white people that Native languages should be saved. We must acknowledge and come to terms with language preservation and oral history. We must understand why these languages matter and how their survival is a testimony to the resilience of humanity in the face of inhuman miseducation meant to save the man by killing the Indian.

It was the beginning of a sense of what the Sierra Club listed as "What's lost and what's left": a yardstick held up for many Americans who had assumed that the wide-open spaces along the trail lay dormant and unthreatened. The bicentennial coincided with the fortieth anniversary of the Wilderness Act. Folks looked around and noticed that there were not that many existing wilderness areas and even fewer pending ones. The bicentennial provided a shot in the arm for conservation and preservation groups who used the attention focused by the commemoration to shine a light on their yardstick. We were shown exactly how much things have changed in the last two hundred years, exactly how much impact we have had on a landscape once one of the most beautiful and fertile on the entire planet. We inevitably asked the question, "Is it too late to get it back?" Trail stewardship is no longer just an afterthought. It has become a number-one priority for many states along the river.

The bicentennial offered people a chance to slow down, to close their eyes and imagine life in a three-miles-per-hour world. They could imagine, "What if it was me? Could I do that?" I have lost count of the number of people I met over the three bicentennial years who sought the opportunity to test themselves, whether by paddling the entire Missouri and Columbia Rivers or by packing up the whole family to do as much of the trail as they possibly could in a two-week shot. These groups were not formal reenactors—they were just doing it for themselves and their love of the expedition.

It was the beginning of a new wave of western art inspired by Lewis and Clark, especially statuary. My favorite would have to be the yet-to-be-completed Confluence Project by Maya Lin. According to her literature, "The Confluence Project is an initiative to reclaim, transform, and reimagine seven places along the historic Columbia River Basin. Through Maya Lin's creative interventions into their history and terrain each site will offer new points of encounter between the natural world and the built environment, the past and the present for people of all backgrounds." Budgeted at twenty-seven million dollars, the nonprofit Confluence Project is scheduled to complete its final site in 2008.

Operas, ballets, and even an aerial ballet troupe put on productions based on Lewis and Clark. One of my favorite titles is a play called *Lewis and Clark reach the Euphrates*. At many places it seemed everyone wanted to get in on the act. As a *Wall Street Journal* reporter disparagingly pointed out, events seemed to be "hijacked by the locals," which might actually explain why they were a success and not a failure, as he tried to imply. Dog owner groups held "Newfie" contests and gardening clubs planted Lewis and Clark and Jefferson gardens. Chautauquas were performed. Music seemed to be a key element: Native American children performed songs about the Corps in their native languages, and symphonies were composed and played by local symphony groups. I think fiddles made the difference in the expedition, and there certainly was no shortage of musical entertainment along the trail in 1804–6.

I am most encouraged about the planting of a seed in many young people's minds that going out into nature is a sublime, as Lewis might say, and wonderful thing and that if we follow the example set by the men and woman of the Corps, there is no limit to the subjects we can study and the answers we can find.

Lately we hear that young people in America are afraid to go outside, too engrossed in their gadgetry to leave the living room, unable to cut the cord to the grid. Psychologists such as Richard Louv nowadays write of "childhoods of imprisonment" and "extinction of experience." They say that even as recently as 1970 children spent the bulk of their recreation time outdoors and still had the freedom to play and explore the natural world with little or no restriction. By 2006 the virtual had replaced the real and we began developing in our children biophobia, a fear of the natural world and ecological processes, thanks to our early-age emphasis on rainforest depletion and endangered species. This can be corrected by encouraging what the psychologists call biophilia, a love of the earth, before we ask them to save it. We need to encourage a sense of well-being in nature. What better way to do that than through the stories of Lewis and Clark?

In my experience the kids who are turned on to Lewis and Clark do not fear things natural. The ones who want to know more about Sacagawea and her son Pomp; Clark's slave, York; and Seaman the dog and their trip to the Pacific know that the place to study this story is outside. And it is because this story took place in the big OUTSIDE and not in a living room or a library that it should always be taught to young people. The more we want to see what the Corps saw and the more we teach our children to value historic and cultural sites, the more voices there will be to speak up for those places. Think of Lewis and Clark as the first Montessori teachers. Think of Sacagawea as an early example of breaking the glass ceiling—she proved to be just as strong and fortuitous as any of her fellow explorers. We cannot afford to stop teaching the important lessons in this story. We can't throw them out with the bathwater of the bicentennial. I would like to challenge the federal, state, and local governments who had anything to do with the commemoration and the interpretive centers, museums, parks programs, and signage to follow up on these beginnings and make sure that the lessons of Lewis and Clark continue to be taught through what we refer to as the "Third Century." We lit the fire with the bicentennial now we must make sure that it does not go out.

I witnessed the profound effect on a youngster of a dip in a hot springs on a cold winter day. I met young homeschooled buckskinners at several events along the trail who were literally chockfull of enthusiasm about Lewis and Clark. "Are you really a Clarkie?" they asked me, and I was surprised that kids would be so discerning. The next time I saw them at the Arch for the final signature event, they firmly shook my hand and showed me their latest period gear, and then serenaded me with songs about Lewis and Clark they had written themselves.

I found myself thinking "If we could just bottle that!" Children aren't afraid to go out into nature, they just need a compelling reason to do so. For many, Lewis and Clark provide that reason. That is a wonderful legacy of the bicentennial, and it will not end after the three years of commemorations are over. It is up to us as parents and educators to continue to be the Corps of Discovery, to continue to encourage the camping trips, the hikes, the nature walks, the float trips, the fishing, yes, and in the name of Theodore Roosevelt, even the hunting. All of those activities that encourage kids to BE IN NATURE. Greenways and soccer fields are not enough. We need to "Pack it in and pack it out" as the saying goes. How can you figure out your place in the world if you have never seen a sky full of stars? A Red Cross volunteer and friend of mine said that in the aftermath of Katrina she camped out with some inner-city kids in an area outside New Orleans that had no power for several nights. It was the first time many of these children had ever seen the stars. One little girl asked her, "Miss Lee Ann, are there stars over New Orleans too?" I think we still need Lewis and Clark to entice kids to look for those stars, to dream about that river, to imagine their own Great Falls. I may be one of the afflicted ones, but I think we still NEED Lewis and Clark, and that the voyage of discovery is really just beginning.

Postscript

Advice to the MSU–Billings
Graduating Class of 2006

It is my distinct pleasure to speak to you today, a day
that marks the passing from one summit of your life to
another, a day signified by pride and a sense of accomplishment and the promise of a shining future yet to
be. I admit I feel a bit out of place giving advice to your
generation. I confess it is a struggle for me to find ways
to advise my own collegian in these uncertain and ever-
challenging times.

When my father was asked to account for the success
of his bestseller *Undaunted Courage*, he used to say it was
because it came out at a time (1996) when Americans
were searching for heroes. To my mind Americans are
constantly searching for heroes, and it seems lately that
we are finding them in the most bizarre places. We
have singing idols and reality show survivors getting as
much ink as the latest nominee for the Supreme Court.
Something seems skewed about our heroes these days.
Yet America is filled with examples of unlikely heroes, the
ones who "git 'er done," as we like to say in Montana.

I would like to speak this morning about living up to promise—of showing the world a clean pair of heels, as my Irish grandpa would say, meaning that if you are in a horse race or a steeplechase, win the race so convincingly all the other horses can see is a pair of heels. I thought I would start with two ordinary and unlikely heroes, at least in my book. They were two men who lived up to an early and absolutely unrepeatable adventure, sort of like your last four years, which many people say were the best and most formative years of their lives. These two men took advantage of the opportunities afforded by that early adventure and made good on the promise of their existence. They went to the moon, in a manner of speaking, and then came back to make the most of their lives through hard work, stick-to-itiveness, and the will to never settle.

Their adventure, of which I am sure you are all familiar, was to accompany the Corps of Northwestern Discovery, otherwise known as the Lewis and Clark Expedition, to the Pacific Ocean and back. George Shannon was a young Kentucky lad of eighteen when he accomplished this mission and is probably most famous, or infamous, for repeatedly getting lost, or separated as his fans like to say, from the main body of the expedition party. Once he even got ahead of the boats thinking he was actually behind them, and because he had no bullets was forced to shoot sticks from his gun and nearly starved to death. During the expedition he managed to earn the respect of his fellow Corps members by honing his hunting skills on the trail. Being the second-to-youngest member of the crew must have made him one of their darlings and no doubt the target of much teasing and hair tousling. But George had the right stuff. His life after the expedition had its ups and downs, but no one could examine it and say he sat around and twiddled his thumbs after returning to the United States. In fact in 1807 Shannon was one of the members of the Corps assigned to return the visiting Mandan chief Sheheke to his villages in present-day North Dakota. During that episode he was wounded in an attack by some Arikara Indians wherein he was shot in the leg, which he later had to have amputated to save his life.

His involvement with the journals of the Lewis and Clark Expedition is important because in 1810 Clark instructed him to assist Nicholas Biddle in editing and organizing the original journals for publication. In a letter recommending Shannon, Clark told Biddle, "George possesses a sincere and undisguised heart, he is highly spoken of by all his acquaintances and much respected at Lexington University where he has been for the last two years." Clark thought so highly of George Shannon that he offered to set him up in a fur-trading business, but George decided to become a judge instead and, ultimately, a member of the House of Representatives and a Kentucky senator. He died at the age of 49 while in court. Even though he chose his own career path, there can be no doubt he made his family and his friend Captain Clark exceedingly proud.

The other youngest member I would like to recall is Jean Baptiste Charbonneau, nicknamed Pomp, also a darling of all of the men, especially of Captain Clark. To be sure, Baptiste, as he came to be called, was but a baby when the expedition occurred, but his presence, along with that of his mother, the Shoshone woman Sacagawea, guaranteed safe passage for the Corps. Other American Indian tribes were unlikely to attack intruders if they traveled with a woman and a child. Perhaps because of his contribution, but surely because of his affectionate regard, Clark named a sandstone formation for him and then memorialized it further by carving his name and the date on it. That signature is the only remaining physical evidence we have of Lewis and Clark's passage through the Louisiana Purchase.

After returning to civilization Clark never forgot his "little dancing boy Baptiste," as he once called him. Three days after saying farewell at the Mandan villages, Clark wrote to Baptiste's parents and offered to adopt the youngest explorer and educate him in St. Louis. This offer was accepted, and Baptiste received a well-rounded education from a Baptist minister in a Catholic Brothers Seminary. Later he was living at a trading village when he met the prince of Germany, who invited him to accompany him back to Europe. With Clark's permission, Baptiste traveled to Germany and eventually to France, England, and North Africa. When he retuned to the United States he went on to become a fur trader, mountain man, and guide who was once said by contemporaries to be the best man on foot in the Rocky Mountains. Baptiste fought in the Mexican War, became a prospector, and then an innkeeper in California. Remarkably, when he died in May 1866 Baptiste was on his way to the gold fields of Montana. According to his obituary in the *Auburn Placer Herald*, Baptiste Charbonneau left California because "the reported discoveries of gold in Montana and the rapid peopling of the territory, excited the imagination of the old trapper and he determined to return to the scenes of his youth." Another obituary described him as "of pleasant manners, intelligent, well read in the topics of the day and was generally esteemed in the community as a good meaning and inoffensive man." I think Clark would agree he lived up to his potential and to the promise of being the littlest explorer on one of the world's most inspiring expeditions.

In my experience with true real-life heroes, of whom I have been lucky enough to meet a few, they share some traits worthy of emulating. They exhibit personal modesty, integrity, and a willingness to share their lifelong love of learning. Most of them would tell you stories of how their accomplishments came about because they were able to summon up the courage to live up to someone's encouraging words, to a dear one's expectations that they can and will do great things. I believe Clark felt that these two youngest explorers could and would live up to their potential in whatever occupation they chose to pursue. As he once told his own son, Meriwether Lewis Clark, who was struggling at West Point at the time, "Try my dear boy to get thro, persevere and show what you can do. On you my son our greatest hopes rest, only perservere my dear boy and you will come out an ornament to the country which gave you burth."

A learned man once said, "The future turns out to be something that you make instead of find. The future is an empty canvas or a blank sheet of paper and if you have the courage of your own thought and your own observation you can make of it what you will."

Being Montanans, either by choice or by birth, full-time or part-time, you are most fortunate. Our state is rife with examples of independent, free-thinking individuals who lived up to their potential and early opportunities: Charles M. Russell, Jeannette Rankin, Bob Marshall, Mike Mansfield, and Dorothy Johnson to name a few. I urge you to study their biographies and follow their examples. They shared a love of our state, a passion for their work, and an unquenchable desire to learn. It is your heritage as citizens of this great state to value place, history, and freedom. Montana has given you a priceless gift, a unique perspective different from any other state's. They call it "The Last Best Place" for a reason. It is a land of infinite opportunity, famous for its big sky, which serves as a constant reminder that we are small and the universe is big, but all things are possible.

And now, thanks to that sheepskin in your hands, you have an obligation to use the gifts you have been given, to honor the advice and to implement what you have learned to help make your community a better place, to do something for the good of your neighbor and for the next generation. Finally, hold on tight to the things that excite your imagination, as George Shannon and Baptiste Charbonneau managed to do. And as my grandfather Tim liked to say, "Now go out there and show the world a clean pair of heels."

Notes

2. MISSOURI RIVER

1. Mullen, *Rivers of Change*, 13.
2. Botkin, *Passage of Discovery*, 9.
3. Jackson, *Letters of the Lewis and Clark Expedition*, 61.
4. Vestal, *The Missouri*, 8, 13, and 52.
5. Catlin, *Letters and Notes*, letter 3.
6. Botkin, *Passage of Discovery*, 9.
7. Fitch, "The Missouri River," 637–38.
8. Young, "That Dammed Missouri River," 412.
9. Fitch, "The Missouri River," 637–38.
10. Moulton, *Journals of Lewis and Clark*, June 21, 1804 (vol. 2); August 5, 1805 (vol. 2).
11. Jackson, *Letters of the Lewis and Clark Expedition*, 223.
12. Jefferson, *Notes on Virginia*, query #2.
13. Least Heat Moon, *River Horse*, 194.
14. Charlevoix, *Historie et description generale de la Nouvelle France*, letter 27.
15. Young, "That Dammed Missouri River," 412.

5. SELECTED AND IMPLANTED BY NATURE

1. Jackson, *Letters of the Lewis and Clark Expedition*, 590.
2. Moulton, *Journals of Lewis and Clark*, June 7, 1805 (vol. 4).
3. Moulton, *Journals of Lewis and Clark*, July 10, 1805 (vol. 4).
4. Moulton, *Journals of Lewis and Clark*, July 27, 1806 (vol. 8).
5. Moulton, *Journals of Lewis and Clark*, April 11, 1806 (vol. 7).
6. Jackson, *Letters of the Lewis and Clark Expedition*, 64.
7. Moulton, *Journals of Lewis and Clark*, August 11, 1805 (vol. 5).
8. Moulton, *Journals of Lewis and Clark*, May 24, 1806 (vol. 7)
9. Jackson, *Letters of the Lewis and Clark Expedition*, 493–494.

6. SUFFICIENTLY AMPLE

1. Jackson, *Letters of the Lewis and Clark Expedition*, 57.
2. Jackson, *Letters of the Lewis and Clark Expedition*, 74.
3. Coues, *History of Lewis and Clark*, vol. 2, 789.
4. Coues, *History of Lewis and Clark*, vol. 2, 818n24.
5. Jackson, *Letters of the Lewis and Clark Expedition*, 375.

7. OPENING OUR EARS

1. Jackson, *Letters of Lewis and Clark Expedition*, 64.
2. Jackson, *Letters of Lewis and Clark Expedition*, 286.
3. McCracken, *George Catlin*, 116.
4. Josephy, *Nez Perce Indians*, 23.
5. Skarsten, *George Drouillard*, 298–301.

8. I GREW HEARTILY TIRED OF THE NATIONAL HUG

1. As this essay is purely speculative, the reader will pardon me for using as many notes as possible to back up my argument.
2. Holmberg, *Dear Brother*, 218.
3. See Attwood's Web site, www.tonyattwood.com.
4. Lawrence Osborne, "The Little Professor Syndrome," *New York Times Magazine*, June 18, 2000, 55–59.
5. Moulton, *Journals of Lewis and Clark*, May 19, 1805 (vol. 4).
6. Moulton, *Journals of Lewis and Clark*, April 25, 1805 (vol. 4).
7. Moulton, *Journals of Lewis and Clark*, May 17, 1805 (vol. 4).

8. Moulton, *Journals of Lewis and Clark*, June 14, 1805 (vol. 4).

9. Moulton, *Journals of Lewis and Clark*, May 31, 1805 (vol. 4).

10. Moulton, *Journals of Lewis and Clark*, July 25, 1806 (vol. 8).

11. Moulton, *Journals of Lewis and Clark*, April 7, 1805 (vol. 4).

12. Jackson, *Letters of the Lewis and Clark Expedition*, 590.

13. Davis, *Francis Walker Gilmer*, 360–361.

14. Meriwether Lewis to Lucy Marks, November 24, 1794, Meriwether Lewis Papers, Missouri Historical Society, St. Louis.

15. Chuinard, "The Court Martial," 12–14.

16. Jackson, *Letters of the Lewis and Clark Expedition*, 180.

17. Dillon, *Meriwether Lewis*, 23.

18. Meriwether Lewis to Lucy Marks, May 22, 1795, Meriwether Lewis Papers, Missouri Historical Society, St. Louis.

19. Moulton, *Journals of Lewis and Clark*, April 7, 1805 (vol. 4).

20. Moulton, *Journals of Lewis and Clark*, July 26, 1806 (vol. 8).

21. Moulton, *Journals of Lewis and Clark*, August 13, 1805 (vol. 5).

22. Jackson, *Letters of the Lewis and Clark Expedition*, 365.

23. Moulton, *Journals of Lewis and Clark*, February 20, 1806 (vol. 6).

24. Graustein, *Thomas Nuttall, Naturalist*, 249–52.

25. Wood and Theissen, eds., *Early Fur Trade*, 238.

26. Jackson, *Letters of the Lewis and Clark Expedition*, 35.

27. Marshall, ed., *The Life and Papers of Frederick Bates*, 109.

28. Moulton, *Journals of Lewis and Clark*, June 14, 1805 (vol. 4).

29. Moulton, *Journals of Lewis and Clark*, July 27, 1806 (vol. 8).

30. Moulton, *Journals of Lewis and Clark*, July 28, 1805 (vol. 5).

31. Marshall, *The Life and Papers of Frederick Bates*, 69.

32. Moulton, *Journals of Lewis and Clark*, August 18, 1805 (vol. 5).

33. Jackson, *Letters of the Lewis and Clark Expedition*, 590.

34. Meriwether Lewis to William Clark, May 29, 1808, William Clark Papers, Missouri Historical Society, St. Louis.

35. Jackson, *Letters of the Lewis and Clark Expedition*, 719–720.

36. Attwood, *Asperger's Syndrome*, 25.

37. Jackson, *Letters of the Lewis and Clark Expedition*, 592.

Bibliography

Ambrose, Stephen E. *Undaunted Courage: Meriwether Lewis, Thomas Jefferson, and the Opening of the American West.* New York: Simon and Schuster, 1996.

Attwood, Tony. *The Complete Guide to Asperger's Syndrome.* Philadelphia: Jessica Kingsley, 2007.

Berman, Morris. *The Reenchantment of the World.* Ithaca NY: Cornell University Press, 1981.

Boorstin, Daniel J. *The Lost World of Thomas Jefferson.* Chicago: University of Chicago Press, 1993.

Botkin, Daniel. *Passage of Discovery: The American Rivers Guide to the Missouri River of Lewis and Clark.* New York: Perigee, 1999.

Brackenridge, Henry M. *Views of Louisiana: Together with a Journal of a Voyage Up the Missouri River in 1811.* Pittsburgh: Cramer, Spear and Eichbaum, 1814.

Catlin, George. *Letters and Notes on the Manners, Customs, and the Conditions of the North American Indians.* 2 vols. London: Privately published, 1841.

Charlevoix, Pierre Francois de. *Historie et description generale de la Nouvelle France.* Paris, 1744.

Chuinard, Eldon G. "The Court Martial of Ensign Meriwether Lewis." *We Proceeded On* 8, no. 4 (Nov. 1982): 12–14.

———. *Only One Man Died: The Medical Aspects of the Lewis and Clark Expedition.* Glendale CA: Arthur Clark, 1979.

Clark, William. William Clark Papers. Missouri Historical Society, St. Louis.

Clarke, Charles G. *The Men of the Lewis and Clark Expedition.* Glendale CA: Arthur Clark, 1970.

Coues, Elliott, ed. *The History of the Expedition Under the Command of Captains Lewis and Clark.* 3 vols. New York: Dover, 1965.

Cutright, Paul. *Lewis and Clark: Pioneering Naturalists.* Urbana: University of Illinois Press, 1969.

Davis, Richard Beale. *Francis Walker Gilmer: Life and Learning in Jefferson's Virginia.* Richmond: Dietz Press, 1939.

Dillon, Richard. *Meriwether Lewis: A Biography.* New York: Coward-McCann, 1965.

Duncan, Dayton. *Out West: American Journey Along the Lewis and Clark Trail.* New York: Viking, 1988.

Fitch, George. "The Missouri River: Its Habits and Eccentricities Described by a Personal Friend." *American Magazine* 53, no. 6 (Apr. 1907): 637–40.

Giuliani, Rudolph. *Leadership.* New York: Miramax Books, 2002.

Golman, Daniel, Richard Boyatzis, and Annie Mckee. *Primal Leadership: Learning to Lead with Emotional Intelligence.* Boston: Harvard Business School, 2002.

Grandin, Temple. *Thinking in Pictures and Other Reports from My Life with Autism.* New York: Doubleday, 1995.

Graustein, Jeannette E. *Thomas Nuttall, Naturalist: Explorations in America, 1808–1841.* Cambridge MA: Harvard University Press, 1967.

Harris, Burton. *John Colter: His Years in the Rockies.* Lincoln: University of Nebraska Press, 1993.

Holmberg, James. J., ed. *Dear Brother: Letters of William Clark to Jonathan Clark.* New Haven: Yale University Press, 2002.

Jackson, Donald Dean. *Letters of the Lewis and Clark Expedition, with Related Documents, 1783–1854.* 2 vols. Urbana: University of Illinois Press, 1962, 1978.

Jefferson, Thomas. *Notes on the State of Virginia*. London: John Stockdale 1787. Reprint, Chapel Hill: University of North Carolina Press, 1955.

Jenkinson, Clay Straus. *The Character of Meriwether Lewis: Completely Metamorphosed in the American West*. Reno: Marmarth Press, 2000.

Josephy, Alvin. *The Nez Perce Indians and the Opening of the Northwest*. Lincoln: University of Nebraska Press, 1979.

Kouzes, James M., and Barry Z. Posner. *The Leadership Challenge*. San Francisco: Jossey-Bass, 2003.

Landeen, Dan, and Allen Pinkham. *Salmon and His People: Fish and Fishing in Nez Perce Culture*. Lewistown ID: Confluence Press, 1999.

Least Heat Moon, William. *River Horse*. Boston: Houghton Mifflin, 1999.

Lewis Meriwether. Meriwether Lewis Papers. Missouri Historical Society, St. Louis.

Louv, Richard. *Last Child in the Woods; Saving Our Children from Nature-Deficit Disorder*. Chapel Hill: Algonquin Books of Chapel Hill, 2006.

Luttig, John. *Journal of a Fur Trading Expedition on the Upper Missouri, 1812–1813*. Edited by Stella Drum. St. Louis: Missouri Historical Society, 1920.

Marshall, Thomas Maitland, ed. *The Life and Papers of Frederick Bates*. St. Louis: Missouri Historical Society, 1926.

McCracken, Harold. *George Catlin and the Old Frontier*. New York: Dial Press, 1959.

Miller, Charles. *Jefferson and Nature: An Interpretation*. Baltimore: Johns Hopkins University Press, 1988.

Moore, Robert, Jr., and Michael Haynes. *Tailor Made and Trail Worn Army Life: Clothing and Weapons of the Corps of Discovery*. Helena: Farcountry Press, 2003.

Moulton, Gary, ed. *The Journals of the Lewis and Clark Expedition*. 13 vols. Lincoln: University of Nebraska Press, 1983–2001.

Mullen, Thomas. *Rivers of Change*. Malibu CA: Roundwood Press, 2004.

Peters, Virginia Roberts. *Women of the Earth Lodges: Tribal Life on the Plains*. Norman: University of Oklahoma Press, 1995.

Prince-Hughes, Dawn. *Songs of the Gorilla Nation: My Journey through Autism.* New York: Harmony Books, 2004.

Rees, John. "The Shoshoni Contribution to Lewis and Clark." *Idaho Yesteryears,* Summer 1958.

Ronda, James P. *Lewis and Clark among the Indians.* Lincoln: University of Nebraska Press, 1984.

Skarsten, M. O. *George Drouillard, Hunter and Interpreter for Lewis and Clark and Fur Trader, 1807–1810.* Glendale CA: Arthur H. Clark, 1964.

Slaughter, Thomas. *Exploring Lewis and Clark: Reflections on Men and Wilderness.* New York: Knopf, 2003.

Thwaites, Rueben Gold, ed. *Original Journals of the Lewis and Clark Expedition, 1804–1806.* 8 vols. New York: Dodd, Mead, 1904–5.

Tubbs, Stephenie Ambrose, and Clay S. Jenkinson. *The Lewis and Clark Companion: An Encyclopedic Guide to the Voyage of Discovery.* New York: Henry Holt, 2003.

Vestal, Stanley. *The Missouri.* New York: Farrar and Rinehart, 1945.

Wood, Raymond W., and Thomas D. Theissen, eds. *Early Fur Trade on the Northern Plains: Canadian Traders among the Mandan Hidatsa Indians 1738–1818.* Norman: University of Oklahoma Press, 1985.

Young, Gordon. "That Dammed Missouri River." *National Geographic* 140, no. 3 (Sept. 1971): 374–412.